Screen Shots

iMac and iBook

iMac and iBook

Virga

First published in the United Kingdom in 2001 by Hachette UK

© English Translation Hachette UK 2001
© Hachette Livre: Marabout Informatique 2000

English translation by Prose Unlimited
Concept and editorial direction: Ghéorghïï Vladimirovitch Grigorieff
Additional research and editorial assistance: Simon Woolf, Rod Cuff, Richard Lucas

A CIP catalogue for this book is available from the British Library

Trademarks/Registered Trademarks

Computer hardware and software brand names mentioned in this book are protected by their respective trademarks and acknowledged. Every effort has been made to make this book as complete and accurate as possible, but the publisher and author cannot accept any responsibility for any loss or inconvenience sustained by any reader as a result of this book's information or advice.

ISBN: 1 84202 038 2

Designed by Graph'M
Layout by M2M
Typeset in Humanist 521
Printed and bound by Graficas Estella, Spain

Hachette UK
Cassell & Co
The Orion Publishing Group
Wellington House
London
WC2R 0BB

Web site: www.marabout.com/Cassell

Table of contents

Chapter I

Introduction

If you've picked up this book and are reading this, you're undoubtedly interested in the iMac or the iBook. You may have just bought one of these fantastic machines or be planning to buy one soon. In either case, you'll find this guide very useful, because the iMac and iBook are not supplied with a full user's manual but with just a slim brochure, and reading the on-line help is not always practical, especially if you're using an iMac for the first time.

This guide will get you started by identifying the essential parts of the iMac and iBook that you'll need day-to-day. In the process, we will also describe the operating system or **OS** (the control program that enables you to use the functions and software associated with the iMac and iBook) and the various peripherals that can be connected to the computer. The right peripherals will help you turn your iMac into a graphics, photography or even recording studio. The iMac really can do it all!

You're obviously not going to become an expert in the iMac just by reading this guide, but we'll get you on your way and enable you to use its functions and to install all the necessary software and peripherals. You'll also know what to do and how to find out more information if a problem arises.

We should point out from the outset that, save in appearance, the iMac and iBook (the portable version) are nearly identical because they use the same basic components (such as the central processor) and the same operating system. Chapter VII covers those topics (such as the trackpad and battery care) that are specific to the iBook.

Happy reading!

A short history...

The iMac did not just descend to us as manna from heaven, though some devotees may well think that is the case. Quite the contrary – in spite of its flashy, futuristic look, it's a worthy descendant of the first Mac computer, the Mac Plus, which was launched by Apple as long ago as 1984. The Mac Plus was the first family computer in the world to use a graphic interface (which incidentally has undergone only minor changes since then). The first version of Mac Plus was monochrome, with only one disk drive and no hard disk. Apple then dropped this all-in-one design for a number of years (although it did market a Mac Plus with a colour monitor in the meantime), but came back to it some ten years later with a new range of products centred around the Performa 5200. This design was highly successful, but was also criticised for its limited expansion possibilities.

The people at Apple didn't rest on their laurels, and in December 1998 unveiled the iMac, the world's first computer designed specifically for intensive Internet use, as well as being the first to jettison the usual dull grey computer casing in favour of snazzy, bright colours. This was a brilliant and successful marketing ploy.

What is the difference between an ordinary computer and a computer for the Internet? In many ways the difference is not that great, except that the latter has no built-in provision for any kind of removable storage device (such as a diskette or a Zip disk), and has a *Setup Assistant* for fast Internet connection. In spite of not having a removable storage unit (which some would consider a handicap), the iMac proved an instant success. Apple proceeded to design an entire family of computers and peripherals around the iMac, including the iBook, the portable version.

The latest high-end, digital-video-oriented model, which came out in 2000, still has no drive for a removable storage device. Many manufacturers, however, offer various storage peripherals (diskettes, Zip or Jaz drives, CD writers, etc.) to boost the iMac and to endow it with all the features of a computer capable of satisfying the most demanding user.

Five generations of iMac

Although still relatively young in computer terms, the iMac has already undergone several updates and has been considerably 'souped up' since the first version of 1998. This book deals with the latest version, marketed at the end of 1999 and revised in July 2000. The latest version of the iBook came out in March 2000.

If you're interested in an older, probably second-hand model, bear in mind that there are several generations of iMac, with the differences between them being not always merely cosmetic. These differences are summarised in the table below.

	iMac Rev A	iMac Rev B	iMac Rev C	iMac Rev D	iMac II	iMac IIDV	iMac IIDVSE	iMac DV+
Processor	G3 233MHz	G3 233MHz	G3 266MHz	G3 266MHz	G3 350MHz	G3 400MHz	G3 400/500MHz	G3 450MHz
RAM	32 MB	32 MB	32 MB	32 MB	64 MB	64 MB	128 MB	64 MB
irDa port	Yes	Yes	No	No	No	No	No	No
Graphic support	ATI Rage IIc 2 MB	ATI RagePro T 6 MB	ATI RagePro T 6 MB	ATI RagePro T 6 MB	ATI RagePro T 8 MB	ATI RagePro T 8 MB	ATI RagePro T 8 MB	ATI RagePro T 8 MB
Storage	4 GB	4 GB	6 GB	6 GB	7 GB	10 GB	13/30 GB	20 GB
CD-ROM	Yes	Yes	Yes	Yes	Yes	Yes	Yes	Yes
DVD	No	No	No	No	No	No	Yes	Yes
FireWire	No	No	No	No	No	Yes	Yes	Yes

The new generation of iMac no longer has an infrared port, but uses the *AirPort* technology explained on page 112. Furthermore, the type of memory (or **RAM**) has also changed (this is important if you plan to add memory to your iMac) and the extension cards are far easier to access. The iMac DV now comes with *iMovie 2*, which is digital film-editing software.

M8492E   iMac 600 MHz 256 MB   40 GB   CDRW   GRAphite.

Additional software

Your iMac/iBook comes with several additional software packages (for Internet, education, games, etc.). Some are installed on your hard disk (in the Applications folder), some need to be installed from CD-ROM. The main software packages are :

Adobe Acrobat Reader

This is a software for reading files created with Adobe Acrobat (files with .pdf extension).

Appleworks 5

This is Macintosh's 'office' suite, incorporating a word processor, a spreadsheet (for preparing accounts) and a database (for organising data and printing reports).

FAXstf

This is fax software for creating a cover page and sending or receiving a fax.

IMovie (only on DV models)

This is the Apple home video software.

Microsoft Internet Explorer and Netscape Communicator

These are Web browsers, used to find and view Web sites on the Internet. Both have similar functionality - it's up to you which one to use.

Microsoft Outlook Express

E-mail management software.

Nanosaur

A game involving dinosaurs.

Quicken Deluxe 2000

A personal finance manager: bank accounts, credit card balances, cash transactions, cheques, etc.

QuickTime 4

This is software for playing digitised video and audio. QuickTime is used on the Internet (as a plug-in) and on many CD-ROMs.

Troubleshooting resources

Here are a few Web sites that could come in handy in case of iMac trouble. These resources provide valuable information, updates and tips concerning extension trouble, freezes, etc.

http://www.macfixit.com

http://www.doctormac.net

http://rescomp.stanford.edu/~scotto/macts.htm

http://www4.coastalnet.com/nccc/Troubleshooting.html

http://forums.xlr8yourmac.com/faq.lasso

Chapter II

Identifying the parts:
Basic hardware and software

Powering up, putting to sleep and shutting down your iMac

There has never been a button on Apple computers to switch the machine on and off. The iMac breaks new ground....

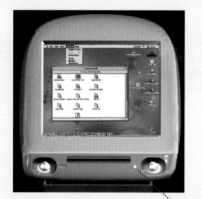

Powering up

Press one of the power buttons:

① At the bottom right of the computer, below the screen;

② On the upper right of the keyboard.

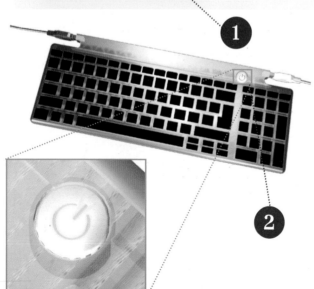

If you won't be using the computer for a while (you can set the length in the appropriate option), you can put your iMac to 'sleep' – put it into low-power mode. You can then 'wake up' your iMac by pressing any key on the keyboard or the mouse button. When your computer is in low-power mode, the small indicator lamp on the power button below the screen turns orange and lights up periodically.

Putting the iMac to sleep

You can put your iMac to sleep in two different ways:

B. Manual method

1. Press a power button. The screen displays the message:
2. Click *Sleep*.

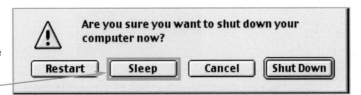

A. Software method

1. Click the *Special* menu.
2. Select *Sleep*.

Shutting down the iMac

A. Software method

1. Click the *Special* menu.
2. Select *Shut Down*.

B. Manual method

1. Press a power button. The screen displays the message:
2. Click *Shut Down*.

Getting to know your iMac

You'll find it useful to take a little time to find your way around your iMac physically, especially at the front, the back and the right-hand side as they conceal very useful connectors.

1
15" monitor
The graphic controller, an ATI RAGE card, is particularly powerful for 2D and 3D graphics (and therefore for games). 8 MB SDRAM video memory.

Three resolution modes:
- 640 x 480
- 800 x 600
- 1024 x 768

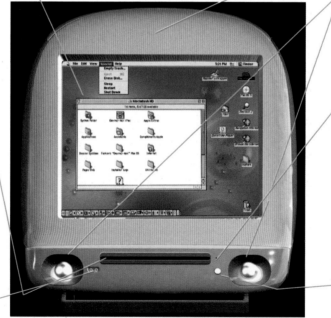

Front

4
Built-in microphone

5
Two stereo speakers

6
CD-ROM manual ejection button (see next page)

2
CD-ROM or (on DV models) DVD drive
This is a slot-fed drive. You simply insert the disk, which is then drawn into the computer. The simplest way to eject the disk is to put its icon in the Trash can (see page 54).

7
Power (and shut-down) button
This button is usually used to power on the computer, or to shut it down (after a menu of options is displayed). The button, which is replicated on the keyboard, can also be used, together with certain keys, to shut down or soft-restart the computer (see page 66).

3
Two ports for analogue headphones
If you have a set of USB headphones, plug them into the USB port to get digital reproduction. These ports can also be used to plug in external speakers.

The infrared port (irDA) which featured on the first iMacs has now disappeared. Instead, Apple has placed an aerial (antenna) round the screen that can be used with the AirPort card (see page 112) for wireless Internet access or to create a wireless local area network (LAN).

Back

Access door for adding more memory or for installing an AirPort card for wireless communication – see page 112.

VGA port

This port (hidden under a cap that can be removed easily with a screwdriver) is available only on the DV models. It is used to connect a VGA monitor (e.g. a 19" screen, so that you can take advantage of the maximum resolution of the iMac) or a TV screen (with a special adapter). The image generated on the screen will be a copy of the image on the iMac screen, not a complementary image as on certain models.

NOTE

The types of memory used by the different generations of iMac/iBook are not the same. If you plan to install extra memory, you must specify your computer model unless your dealer is installing it for you.

CD-ROM or DVD frozen

If your computer refuses to start and you have to use the operating system CD-ROM to reinstall programs, there may already be a CD-ROM or DVD disk in the drive. To eject it, you can use a very simple 'low-tech' method. Take a paperclip, straighten it, insert it into the tiny hole located on the right of the disk slot, and press; the disk in the drive will be ejected.

Right side

This is the most interesting part of the iMac because it contains all the ports needed to expand the system. Each port is identified by an icon.

② Analogue audio input port
This port is used to connect an external microphone having a better quality than that of the computer's built-in microphone.

① Analogue audio output port
This port is used to plug in external speakers, for example. (Note that if you want digital quality, you should use a USB port instead.)

③ Two FireWire ports
These ports are used to connect digital devices (still or video cameras) as well as other peripherals that require high transfer speeds (such as certain high-end hard disks, for instance). They are available only on the iMac DV.

FireWire

FireWire is a high-speed two-way serial bus (also known as IEEE 1394 or iLink). This port is used to plug and unplug peripherals – up to 63 on the same port! – without switching the computer off.

The FireWire cable is extremely fine, but can nonetheless carry sound, video, images and auxiliary data (e.g. the time code needed to synchronise the video). This port was invented by Apple but is now used by all manufacturers in the digital video and photo sector, as well as acting as a connection to hard disks and other peripherals that require high speed. This bus is available on the iMac DV series models only (which are also delivered with the iMovie software application for creating digital videos).

Internal modem port

The internal modem is a latest-generation 56kbps modem (V90 or k56flex). You'll need to connect the modem port to a telephone outlet by means of the cable supplied for that purpose in the iMac box. You can then use the modem to connect to a network or the Internet, to send or receive faxes, etc.

USB ports

These are used to connect most peripherals, including the printer, modem, keyboard and mouse (which is connected to one of the keyboard's USB ports). You can then use these peripherals immediately. USB ports are also used on the most recent PCs, so most peripherals are now compatible on the two platforms (with the right software in use, of course).

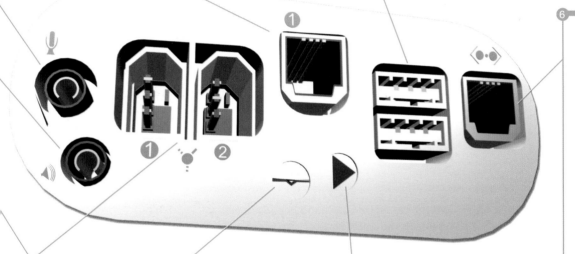

Ethernet port

This port has numerous functions. It is used to connect to a local area network, a printer, a cable modem or ADSL. It is also used to share files between two computers. The Ethernet port automatically recognises the transmission speed and is therefore 10BaseT and 100BaseT compatible. You can network several computers (Macs and PCs) with it. The Ethernet port connector looks very much like a modem connector, so take care not to confuse them (just as you shouldn't confuse Ethernet with the Internet!).

Programmer's button

This button is intended for use by programmers to test program routines.

Restart button

Press this button when the computer has frozen and you cannot get it to work again by any other means.

The keyboard

Until recently, the keyboard supplied with the iMac was rather small and not very comfortable, especially if you're used to other Macintosh keyboards.

Fortunately, you can always connect your iMac to another keyboard, provided it has a **USB** port (so an old Mac keyboard will not do). Furthermore, from October 2000 the iMac has been delivered with a new and more comfortable extended keyboard.

In addition to the two **USB** ports, the keyboard also features the power on / shut down button (with a functional duplicate found below the screen). Some keys have a specific purpose and are briefly described here:

The **Caps Lock key** is the only one that lights up when enabled. It converts into upper case (capitals) any letter of the alphabet that you type, until you press the Caps Lock key again. It does not affect numerals or punctuation marks.

When you hold down one of the two **Shift keys**, any alphabetic letter you type is shifted to upper case; and if you press any key having two different symbols etched on it, the upper symbol is used.

The **Control key**, the **Alt** (or **Option**) **key** and the **Command key** (the key with an Apple on it) are used in conjunction with other keys to perform special commands or to obtain special characters (see pages 64 – 66).

The USB keyboard itself has two USB ports which are fed by the bus, i.e. directly from the computer, and which can be used to connect peripherals. As these connectors are powered directly from the bus, they can be used only to connect peripherals with low power consumption such as a mouse or a disk drive, or peripherals powered by an external source.

The **@** (at-sign) key is used in e-mail addresses.

The **Return key** is the largest on the keyboard. Its function depends on the software being used. In the operating system, it activates the currently-selected button in a dialogue box.

The **Num key** turns the smaller group of keys on the right into a numeric pad (otherwise, this group of keys can be used to move the cursor, although the cursor movement symbols are not etched on the keytops).

The **Help key** is used to open the Help menu (see page 62).

The **Space bar** is the longest key on the keyboard. Its function depends on the software being used, but it usually inserts a blank space between typographic characters.

The **Enter key** is on the numeric pad. Its function depends on the software being used. In the operating system, it activates the currently-selected button in a dialogue box. In certain software applications (such as Microsoft Word, for example) it performs a different function from that of the Return key.

Certain keys must be pressed simultaneously to unfreeze the computer (see page 66). Some key combinations are also used for shortcuts (see pages 64 and 65).

Getting a grip on the mouse

The iMac mouse has only one button, which always comes as a surprise to **PC** users who are used to two, three or even more buttons. For the record, the inventor of the mouse (Douglas Engelbart, 1969) sold his patent for the paltry sum of **US $10,000**. An ingenious inventor but not so good as a businessman!

You can perform three types of action with the iMac mouse:

1. Click

A single click consists of pressing the button rapidly and then releasing it. A click is normally used to select an item.

2. Double-click

A double-click consists of pressing the button rapidly twice without moving the mouse. You usually double-click to launch a program.

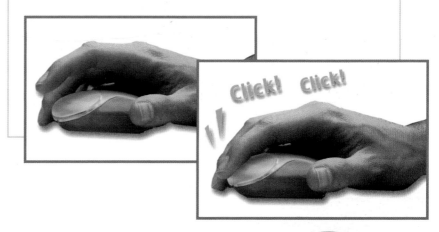

The mouse controls a cursor on the screen. The cursor's shape varies depending on the operation you're performing (something you'll discover as you use your computer).

3. Drag and drop

This indispensable technique might take some practice before you get the hang of it.

1. Position the cursor on a given item, such as a file.
2. Hold down the mouse button.
3. Drag the cursor to where you want to 'drop' the object.
4. Release the mouse button.

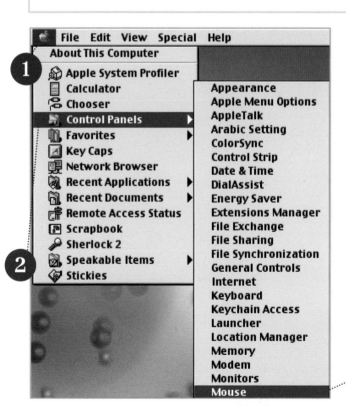

To adjust the mouse tracking and double-click speed to your liking, all you have to do is:

1. Open the *Apple* menu.
2. Choose *Control Panels*.
3. Select *Mouse* and change the settings.

TIP

Before you drop items into a folder (see page 40) you may want to look at the contents of that folder. If you don't release the button immediately in step 3.3 above, the folder will be opened. If you then decide you don't want to drop the new material into it, keep the mouse button held down and drag the cursor out of the folder (which will then close automatically).

The iMac screen

Everything starts with the iMac screen, which gives you access to all the objects on the computer at a (double) click of the mouse. The operating system is already installed on the iMac, and the first screen (shown below) displays various items:

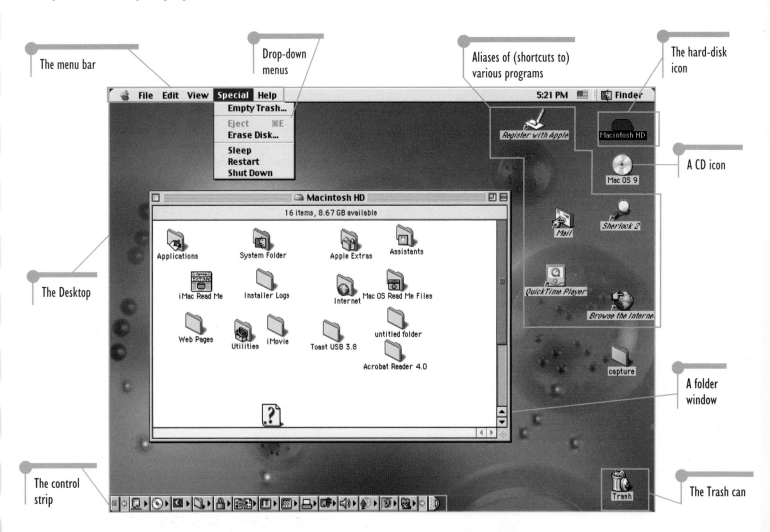

The menu bar

Drop-down menus

Aliases of (shortcuts to) various programs

The hard-disk icon

A CD icon

The Desktop

A folder window

The control strip

The Trash can

1 Menu bar

The menu bar is the anchor for several menus, which differ depending on the application. When you click on a menu, it drops down to offer various command options and/or submenus.

Note

Some commands in the menu bar and in the pull-down menus are greyed (dimmed) at times. This means that they are not available for the selected object at that time. For instance, if you select the hard-disk icon, the Appearance command is not available.

2. Control strip

The control strip is composed of several icons dedicated to the essential functions of the iMac. A small menu pops up when you click on an icon.

3. Desktop

The Desktop is the graphical command centre of your iMac. You'll use it to run programs and execute OS commands such as *Copy* and *Delete*. You can also place various documents and programs on it. Very bare at the outset, the Desktop can get cluttered very quickly. If you don't like the way your Desktop looks or is organised, you can always customise it quickly and easily (see page 68).

4. Trash can

The *Trash can* is used to store files temporarily before you delete them permanently, but you can also use it to eject a diskette, CD-ROM or similar storage device by dragging the appropriate icon on to it.

5. Hard disk

It's called *Macintosh HD* by default, but you can give it any name you want (here it's called *VIRGA*). It contains all your programs and documents, organised in folders and files. To open the hard disk and view its contents, simply double-click on its icon.

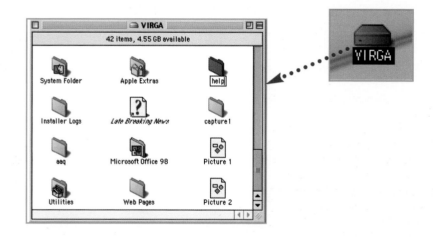

6. Aliases

Aliases are shortcuts (represented by icons) that point to other files; they are duplicates of existing icons. An alias is positioned in a more convenient location than the original icon – for example, on the Desktop. Double-clicking on the alias produces the same result as double-clicking on the original icon, without having to search for the original.

The differences between an alias and the original icon are that:
• its file name is in italics.
• it can be deleted without the original file being affected.
• it takes up very little disk space (because it is nothing more than an icon).

You create an alias by selecting the original and going to the *File/Make alias* menu item (or just *Command + M*).

iMac basic vocabulary

To understand properly, you have to speak the lingo. More than 10,000 IT-related words have now entered the language, but we can get a long way with about a dozen.

Alias
 An icon representing a shortcut to a graphic object (such as a file or folder), used to access a file quickly from several locations on the disk without having to duplicate the whole file.

Application
A software program that performs a specific set of tasks or functions: examples include word processors, spread-sheet handlers and graphic software.

Desktop
A metaphor used to portray the screen background, the primary view of your computer containing the icons that are most important for you. The *Finder*, *Application*, *Keyboard* and other such menus are displayed on it. The Desktop can be customised to your wishes, requirements, tastes, state of mind, etc.

Dialogue box
A window that pops up on the screen containing options, lists of objects, etc. for you to choose from.

Drop-down menu
A menu that appears on the screen when you click on certain sensitive areas.

File
 An organised set of data stored on a magnetic medium (such as a hard disk). Programs, texts, spreadsheets, graphics etc. are stored as files.

Finder
 Finder is the graphical interface of the Macintosh operating system, through which a user carries out most of the day-to-day operations (copy, paste, format, etc.).

Folder
A group of related files or other folders that you can refer to by a single name or an associated icon.

Icon
A small graphic symbol used to represent an application, a folder or a file. To use an application represented by an icon, simply point to it with the mouse cursor and double-click.

Item
 Any object that is part of the user interface: an icon, an image, a window, a sound, etc.

Window
The basic unit of a graphic interface. A rectangular area of the screen is used to display icons, graphics, text or anything else visual produced by an application. You can usually adjust the size and position of a window to suit your needs.

Mac OS

The Mac OS (operating system) is the nerve centre of your computer. It controls not only the computer's internal operations but also all inputs to and outputs from the peripherals. In a word, it's simply indispensable.

The latest version of Mac OS is version 9. Your iMac or iBook, however, may come with an older version (for example 8.6) if you are buying second-hand. You can keep this version, of course, but it is best to ask your dealer (or Apple directly via their Web site) for an update. Note that an update can sometimes have disadvantages. For example, each new version takes up more disk space and may have new features that are incompatible with some older programs. At times, a device driver has to be changed too. So don't be too alarmed if a program or peripheral that ran flawlessly under Mac OS 8.6 refuses to work properly under Mac OS 9. If this happens, you probably need to obtain an update of the program in question or to install a new driver for the peripheral (drivers are available free of charge on the manufacturer's Web site).

Mac OS version 9, the version discussed in this book, is definitely worth installing because of its many new features, which we shall mention here for readers who are familiar with previous versions.

New features in MAC OS 9

The most interesting of these many new features concern the Internet and security.

•
•
•

For the Internet

1 *Sherlock*, the search utility, has been updated to version 2.

2 The iMac can be turned into a file server.

3 The iMac can be operated by remote control (using **TCP/IP**) via the Internet.

4 Programs can be updated automatically.

5 You can search the Internet automatically.

The search utility *Sherlock*.

... For security

1 Several users (up to 40) can use the same Mac.

2 It is easy to create 'keychains' in which you can safely store all your passwords.

3 You can use your voice as your password.

4 Your data can be encrypted.

A modern operating system is composed of a set of extremely powerful modules. If any one of them fails, you will not be able to use some of the functions of the operating system, and you will have to reinstall **MAC OS** from the relevant **CD-ROM** (see page 149).

As far as the new user is concerned, what you need to know about the operating system boils down essentially to learning how to use the *Finder* (see next page). You'll need to know more about the operating system later (such as how to install new fonts or share your iMac), but you can learn what you need to know as you go along by following the explanations provided in the *Help* menus.

Important note

Never mix items from different versions of the operating system.

The Finder

The *Finder* is the most important program on your computer, running constantly as a background task. You'll use it to organise your Desktop, to run applications, to discover the characteristics of your iMac, to shut the computer down and for many other things. The *Finder* is the first program displayed on the screen when you switch on your iMac. You can go back to it at any time by clicking the *Applications* menu (upper right corner of the screen) and then selecting *Finder*.

The *Finder* is the visible part of the Macintosh operating system. The standard *Finder* contains nine elements:

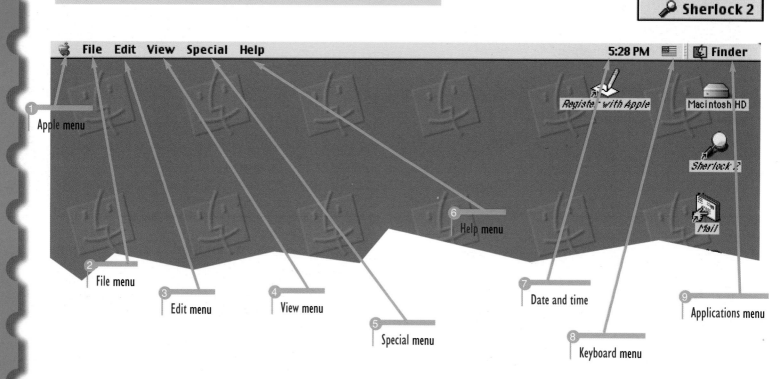

1 Apple menu
2 File menu
3 Edit menu
4 View menu
5 Special menu
6 Help menu
7 Date and time
8 Keyboard menu
9 Applications menu

The Finder's menus

1 Apple Menu

This has two functions. You can use it to:

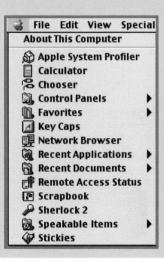

A. Obtain information about the program in use.

B. Run an application (some applications are added to this menu by the system, but you can add more yourself as you please (see page 138).

2. File Menu

This is the most important menu for handling the basic components of your computer such as disks, folders and documents.

3. Edit Menu

This has three essential functions. You can use it to:

A. Set your *Finder* preferences.

B. Display the contents of the clipboard (see page 78).

C. Carry out various operations on documents (such as *Cut* and *Paste*).

4. View Menu

You can use this to select the view modes in the Desktop and in windows.

5. Special Menu

From this menu you can carry out some basic operations such as ejecting disks, shutting down the computer and emptying the *Trash can*.

6. Help Menu

You can use this menu to get help with your questions.

There is a simplified version of the Finder that shows only the most important commands. To activate (and deactivate) the Simple Finder, go to the Finder's Preferences window, and:

1. Click the Edit Menu.

2. Click Preferences.

3. Click the General tab.

4. Tick Simple Finder.

7. Date and time

5:32 PM Click the time display to switch to the date display, and vice versa.

8. Keyboard Menu

This menu (which may not be present in your particular installation) is used to tell the **MAC OS** that you're changing keyboards.

9. Applications Menu

When several applications are open at the same time, you can use this menu to switch between programs or to go back to the *Finder* at any time.

Some basic operations carried out from the Finder

If an application such as your word processor is open, go to the *Applications* menu and click *Finder*. Note that you can carry out most *Finder* operations directly from the keyboard. In general, you use the *Command* key in conjunction with another key (see page 65).

Duplicate a file

You'll find it's often useful to make a copy of a file, just to be safe. The file will be duplicated in the same window – and have the same name – as the original, but *Finder* will add the word 'copy'. To duplicate a file, select it, click the *File* menu (in the *Finder*) and then click *Duplicate* (or use the keyboard shortcut *Command + D*).

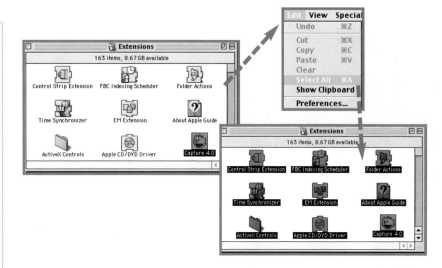

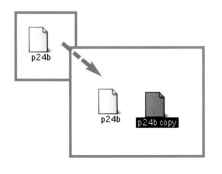

Select all files in a folder

You may want to select all the files in a folder at a single click (in order to copy them to another folder, for example). Click in the window from which you want to select all the files. In the *Finder*, select the *Edit* menu and then *Select All* (*Command + A*).

Open a new folder

We open a new folder every time we want to regroup certain items. In the *Finder*, select the *File* menu, click *New Folder* (*Command + N*), then give a name to the new folder.

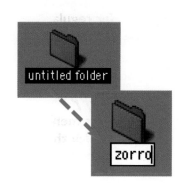

Print the window

In the *Finder*, select the *File* menu and click *Print Window*. The program will print the contents of the active window.

Eject a disk

To eject a disk, select it, open the *Special* menu and click *Eject* (*Command + E*). If the disk is not ejected, that's because one of the items on it (at times simply a character font) is still being used by an application. In such a case, you must close the application first.

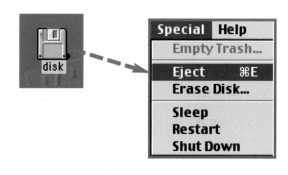

The Apple menu and the control panels

We'll refer regularly to the *Apple* menu and the *control panels* in this book. So it is worth having a closer look at these indispensable features of your iMac.

1. The Apple menu

To access this menu, you simply click the Apple icon at the upper left-hand corner of your screen.

This menu is there to make working with your iMac easier. You can use it to:

① Gain immediate access to an object (application, folder, document, image, etc.).

② Obtain information about a program in use.

③ Find a recently used document or recently opened application.

Adding an object to the *Apple* menu is child's play:

① Open the *System* folder.

② Locate *Apple Menu Items*.

③ Drag the object of your choice on to this icon (this can be an alias).

2. The control panels

These form the strategic centre of your iMac. You'll return to them time and again in order to enter settings or to configure your computer.

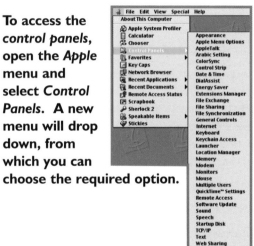

To access the *control panels*, open the *Apple* menu and select *Control Panels*. A new menu will drop down, from which you can choose the required option.

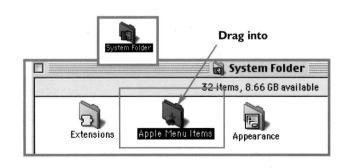

Drag into

Formatting a storage medium

To use a software application properly, you must first be able to format a storage medium for it. Some such media (diskettes, Zip drives, hard disks, etc.) are often preformatted, but they are usually intended for **PCs**; so you will have to (re)format them as if they were blank. Most Macintosh computers can read **PC** disks, but not all users have installed the software modules needed for this purpose, so it's best to use Macintosh-formatted media.

Remember that because different formatting is needed for the Macintosh and for the PC, you will usually have to run the formatting routine.

1. Formatting a diskette

Obviously, you can perform this operation only if your iMac has a diskette (floppy disk) drive. A diskette drive is very inexpensive and we strongly advise you to buy one. Working without a back-up drive is living dangerously indeed (what will you do, for instance, if an important personal file is accidentally erased?), not to mention forgoing a truly universal communication tool.

To format a diskette, go to *Finder* and:

① Select the diskette icon.

② Click the *Special* menu.

③ Choose *Erase Disk*.

④ In the new menu, select *MAC OS Standard*.

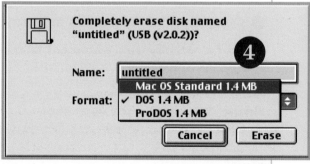

2. Formatting a Zip (or Jaz) drive

You'll first need to install the **Tools** application supplied (usually on **CD-ROM**) with your Zip drive. This application then features several formatting options.

You can also format diskettes for the PC with your iMac, and then use them to copy iMac files (such as text or images) that can be read on any PC.

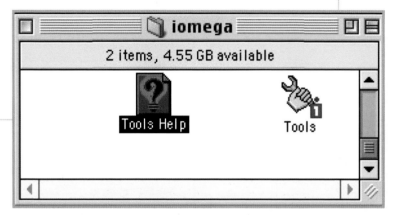

3. Formatting the hard disk

The hard disk is factory formatted, so you will need to (re)format it only if you experience serious problems that cannot be solved either with the troubleshooting application delivered with the iMac or with **Norton Utilities** (a program readily available on the market). Before you format a hard disk, ask an experienced user to save its contents, which will otherwise definitely be lost during the formatting process.

As a novice user, you should refrain from formatting and repair procedures. If real problems occur, reinstall the operating system from the **CD-ROM** delivered with the computer (or from one with a more recent **OS** version).

Configuring function keys

You can make your software easier to run by configuring each of the twelve function keys to perform a specific operation. For example, you can use the function keys to run programs such as *Sherlock* (search) or the *Calculator*.

To configure the keys:

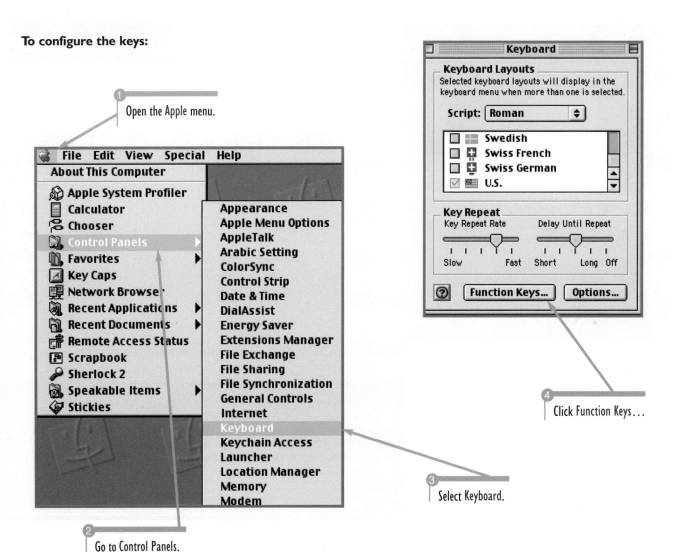

① Open the Apple menu.

② Go to Control Panels.

③ Select Keyboard.

④ Click Function Keys...

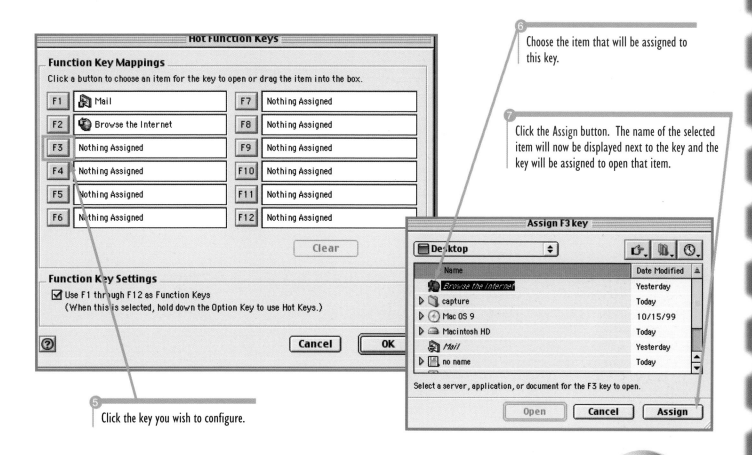

Choose the item that will be assigned to this key.

Click the Assign button. The name of the selected item will now be displayed next to the key and the key will be assigned to open that item.

Click the key you wish to configure.

Note

Some programs that act directly on the system have priority over the function keys.

These programs are not identified in the function key mappings, so you'll find it safer and more useful at times to combine the function keys with the Option key as indicated below:

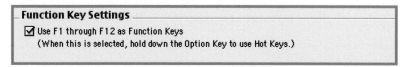

Chapter III

Getting started with the iMac

Files and Folders

A file is an organised set of data stored on a magnetic medium (such as a diskette or hard disk) under a specific name. Programs, texts, spreadsheets, graphics, photographs and so on are stored as files. The icon representing the file is often specific and reflects the nature of the file (Excel spreadsheet, Word document, Photoshop image, etc.).

Here are
a few file samples

A folder is a group of related files or other folders that you can refer to by a single name or associated icon. As key components for organising your data, folders are indispensable, when you consider that a hard disk can contain thousands of files of all kinds. By enabling you to create as many folders as you wish, the operating system helps you organise your hard disk and make your work easier and more productive.

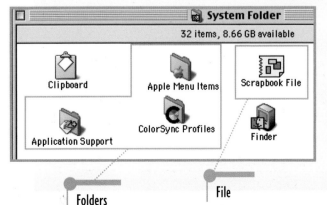

Folders   File

- Folders contain files but can also contain other folders.
- When you open a file, you usually run a software program that can read the contents of that file.
- When you open a folder, you really open a window that lets you see what files are within the folder (see page 43).
- The operating system treats folders essentially like files – so they can be copied, deleted, etc.

1. Creating a new file

Files are usually created by applications. For example, a word processor creates text files, a spreadsheet program creates spreadsheet files and an image retouching program creates image files. To create a file, most software programs use the *Save* or *Save As* command.

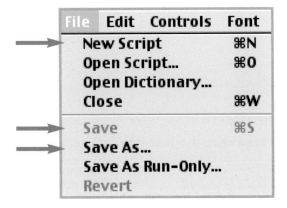

Each new folder will initially be named untitled folder #, where # will depend on the number of folders for which you have not yet assigned names, because no two items in the same window can have exactly the same name. So if you create several folders one after the other (in the same window), their names will be untitled folder 1, untitled folder 2, untitled folder 3 and so on.

2. Creating a new folder

To create a new folder, open the *File* menu and choose *New Folder*. We can create a folder at any logical level we wish; but as we've not yet described how windows are organised, we'll create our new folder on the Desktop (using the *Finder*, of course):

1. Open the *File* menu.
2. Select *New Folder*.
3. The *Finder* creates a new folder initially named *untitled folder 1*.
4. To rename the folder, click the name (not the icon), and key in the new name.

3. Managing the items in a folder

The items in a folder can be renamed (see page 41), selected one at a time or all together (see page 51), moved by dragging and dropping (see page 21) or deleted (see page 54).

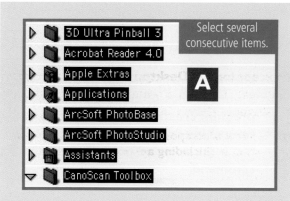

Select several consecutive items.

4. Selecting items in a folder

A. To select an item, click its icon.

B. To select all the items in the open folder, use the keyboard shortcut *Command + A.*

C. To select several consecutive items, click on an empty area near the first item of the list, and then drag the cursor to the last item of the list.

D. To select several non-consecutive items, click the first item you wish to select, hold down the *Shift* key and click the other items you want. When you have finished your selection, release the *Shift* key.

Regardless of how you selected the items, you can always deselect one or more of them. Simply hold down the Shift key and click the item(s) you wish to deselect.

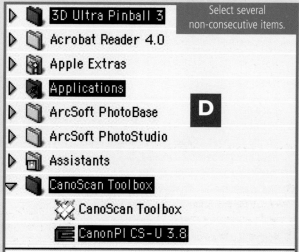

Select several non-consecutive items.

Working with windows

Except for the Desktop, which is a special window, all iMac items are displayed in windows that follow the same rules. To open a window, you simply click its icon. For example, if we double-click the iMac hard-disk icon, the window shown below will open.

This window is composed of the following items, found in nearly every window (including application windows):

Close box
Click this box to close the window. If it's an application window and you've not saved your current work, the program will ask whether you want to save it.

Title bar
The title bar contains the window's name.

Get info
This area (not found in all windows) contains information on the window's contents.

Zoom box
Click this box to enlarge the window to its maximum size; click a second time to return it to its previous size.

Collapse box
Click this box to shrink your window to its title bar; click a second time to expand it again.

Scrollbar
This bar appears when the window is too small to display all its contents.

Scroll box
This box is used to scroll a window (remember that documents may run to hundreds of screens). To scroll horizontally, click the scroll box, hold down the mouse button and slide the box.

Scroll areas
These areas are situated around the window except for the title-bar area. Click a scroll area, hold down the button, move the mouse on the mouse pad and the window will move accordingly.

Size box
The size box is used to change the window's height or width.

Scroll arrows
Click these arrows to scroll line by line in the window.

Viewing windows

The items in a window can be viewed in different ways (modes), which may help you find a particular item more rapidly. Three views are available:

1. As Icons

This is the standard, no-nonsense view mode. Remember that each icon should be displaying a typical image for the item it represents. If this is not the case, you must reinitialise the **PRAM** (see page 145).

TIPS

• Double-click the title bar to collapse the window. (This feature must be activated in the Appearance control panel under Options.)

• Hold down the Command key as you click the title bar to reveal the location of the file within the folders on the system.

2. As Buttons

This view mode is for beginners. The buttons cannot be moved, so you cannot delete a file accidentally. Furthermore, when you view items as buttons, a simple click is all it takes to open a folder or run an application.

3. As List

This is the most interesting view mode because it provides a lot of useful information. For instance, you can view the items below:

Click the title to sort items according to the ordering implied by that title.

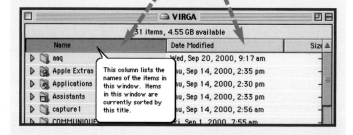

Sorting window contents

A. Sorting

To sort the contents of a window in order
to get a clearer view of the items it contains:

1. Open the *View* menu.

2. Select *as List*.

3. Go back to the
View menu.

4. Select *View
Options*.

5. Tick all the columns
in *Show Columns*.

6. Click *OK*.

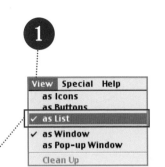

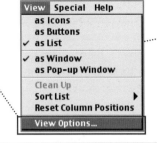

The items are now shown as a list, and you can proceed to sort
each column. Click the header of the column: the items are
sorted immediately according to the ordering implied by the
title of that column (name, date modified, date created, etc.).

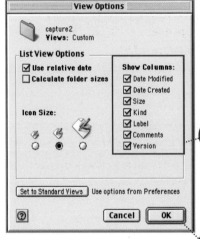

B. Reversing the sort order

To change the sort order in
a window from ascending to
descending or vice versa,
click the arrow icon above
the right scrollbar.

C. Cleaning up

If your filing has become untidy,
with scattered or overlapping icons,
activate the window and select the
View/Clean Up menu item. You can
automatically rearrange those files
in neat rows and columns.

TIP

To open a folder at
the same time as
closing the window in
which its icon is displayed,
hold down the Alt key while
double-clicking the icon.

Arranging and closing windows

When a window is closed, it disappears from the screen and its icon returns to its original location.
The window's items can be arranged according to various criteria using the *View* command in the menu bar.

The best way to find a document rapidly is to sort all documents in the window according to the most significant criterion: file name, date created, type etc.

To close a window, click the *Close* box.

To close all the open windows, hold down the *Alt* key and click the *Close* box.

The active window is always shown in the foreground. Passive windows are in the background and their title bars are greyed. To activate a window, simply click anywhere within it: the window will now be shown in the foreground and the title bar will no longer be greyed.

Pop-up window

Pop-up windows are a new feature of the iMac (MAC OS version 8.5) and are used to free space on the screen while keeping the main windows literally at your fingertips.

Creating a pop-up window: Method 1

1. Open a window.
2. Click the *Collapse* box.
3. Drag the window title to the bottom of the screen.
4. The window is now deactivated and only the window tab is visible.
5. Click the tab to open the window.

LANGUAGES	
	2 items, 4.55 GB available

NOTE
To remove the pop-up effect, move the tab to the top of the screen. Pop-up windows do not reappear on start-up (i.e. they disappear once the system is shut down).

Creating a pop-up window: Method 2

1. Open a window.
2. Select the *View* menu.
3. Click *as Pop-up Window*.
4. Click the window tab; the window is moved to the bottom of the screen.
5. Click outside the window to reduce the window to a tab.
6. Click the tab to open the window.

View	Special	Help
✓ as Icons		
as Buttons		
as List		
as Window		
✓ as Pop-up Window		
Clean Up		
Arrange		▶
Reset Column Positions		
View Options...		

Icons

The iMac uses a graphic interface. This means that most items are represented by icons. Each application (or program) has its own icon, but there are generic icons you should get to know. You double-click an icon to open it – that is, to execute a command on the object represented by the icon. This would launch a program or open a hard disk, for instance.

Each icon has a caption. To rename an icon, click the name (not the icon), select the name, delete it (with the ⌫ key) and enter the new name. If you change your mind, press *Esc* immediately. Here are a few standard icons:

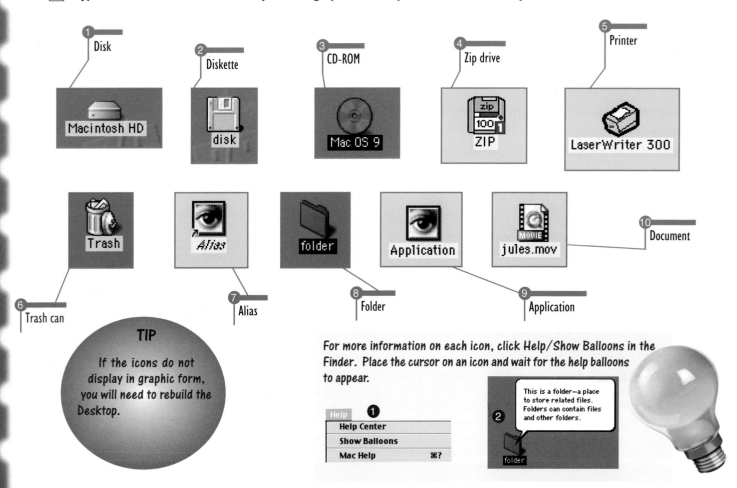

TIP

If the icons do not display in graphic form, you will need to rebuild the Desktop.

For more information on each icon, click Help/Show Balloons in the Finder. Place the cursor on an icon and wait for the help balloons to appear.

Help ❶
Help Center
Show Balloons
Mac Help ⌘?

❷ This is a folder—a place to store related files. Folders can contain files and other folders.

folder

Menus

As already mentioned in the section on the *Finder* menus, everything starts with a menu. We have also seen the *Apple* menu (page 33) and the *Applications* menu, which let you return to the *Finder* (page 28) at all times and switch between applications. We'll also discover keyboard shortcuts for using menus and their options without using the mouse (page 64).

Let's now take a closer look at the *Applications* menu and the treasures hidden in contextual menus.

1. The Applications menu

Each application that you open is added to the *Applications* menu, so you can switch rapidly between applications using this menu.

To switch from the active application to another application, you simply select the latter in the menu. The application's icon appears in the upper right-hand corner and the menu is displayed on the screen.

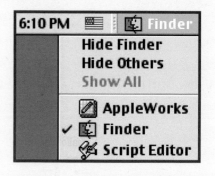

All these applications are open.

To make things easier, you can turn the Applications menu into a window.

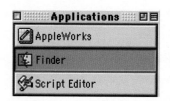

Open the Applications menu, hold down the mouse button and drag it. A window will open containing the icons of all the open programs. It's known as the Application Selector.

2. Contextual menus

As their name indicates, contextual or context menus vary depending on the context, i.e. on the item selected. There are very many contextual menus, because nearly every item, including the Desktop, has its own such menu. You can use contextual menus to gain fast access to commands related to the selected item.

TIP

To open a contextual menu, hold down the Ctrl key and click the relevant item. To close it again, click outside the menu.

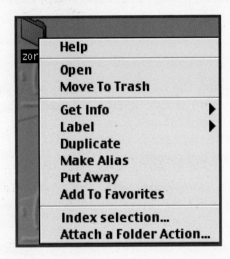

| Help |
| Open |
| Move To Trash |
| Get Info ▶ |
| Label ▶ |
| Duplicate |
| Make Alias |
| Put Away |
| Add To Favorites |
| Index selection... |
| Attach a Folder Action... |

Accessing contextual menus

1 Press the *Ctrl* key; a new icon will appear next to the cursor.

2 Select an item for which you want a contextual menu.

3 A menu of options is shown for you to select from.

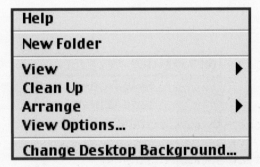

| Help |
| New Folder |
| View ▶ |
| Clean Up |
| Arrange ▶ |
| View Options... |
| Change Desktop Background... |

If no item is selected, the contextual menu will show the commands that relate to the open window or to the Desktop.

If several items are selected, the menu contains commands that can apply to all of them.

Learning to select

There are many ways of selecting items, and mastering them will make your work a lot easier. A selected item is darkened and its name is shown in reverse video.

1. To select an item

Click the item.

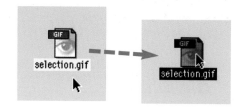

2. To select multiple non-consecutive items

Hold down the *Shift* key and click each of the items.

3. To select several consecutive items

Click next to an item, hold down the mouse button and move it to include the items in the selection frame (the selected items are easily identifiable because they change colour).

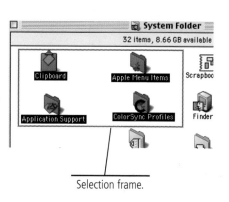

Selection frame.

4. To select all the items in a window

Go to *Finder*, open the *Edit* menu and choose *Select All*. You can also use the shortcut combination *Command + A*.

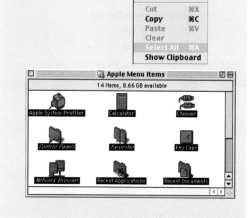

Basic file operations

The basic operations on files (and folders) apply to all operating systems: copy, duplicate, delete, move, etc. All these operations can be carried out very easily using the mouse and/or a contextual menu.

A. Using the contextual menu

❶ **Select an application file (such as Word).**

❷ **Press *Ctrl*.**

❸ **The following contextual menu is displayed:**

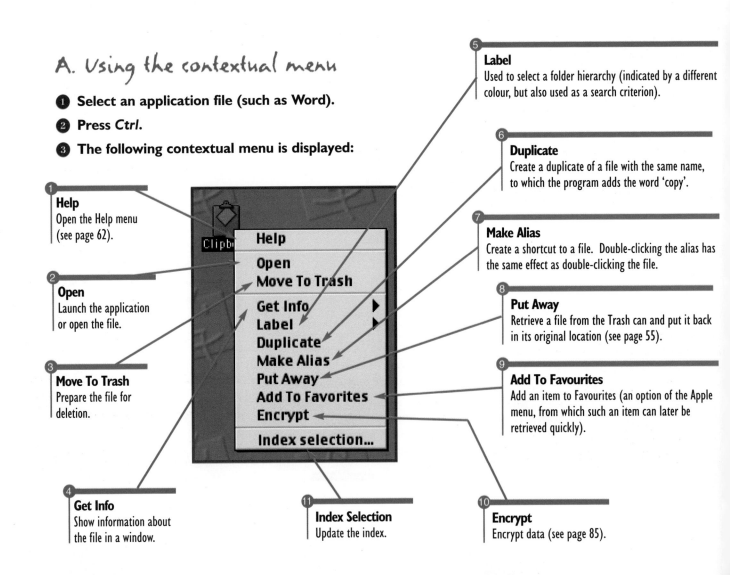

Help
Open the Help menu
(see page 62).

Open
Launch the application
or open the file.

Move To Trash
Prepare the file for
deletion.

Get Info
Show information about
the file in a window.

Index Selection
Update the index.

Encrypt
Encrypt data (see page 85).

Label
Used to select a folder hierarchy (indicated by a different
colour, but also used as a search criterion).

Duplicate
Create a duplicate of a file with the same name,
to which the program adds the word 'copy'.

Make Alias
Create a shortcut to a file. Double-clicking the alias has
the same effect as double-clicking the file.

Put Away
Retrieve a file from the Trash can and put it back
in its original location (see page 55).

Add To Favourites
Add an item to Favourites (an option of the Apple
menu, from which such an item can later be
retrieved quickly).

B. Using the mouse

You will still have to use the mouse to move files between folders.

If you drag the solitary file contained in **Folder A** and drop it into **Folder B**, **Folder A** will now be empty and the file will be in **Folder B** (the file has been moved).

However, if you drag the solitary file contained in **Folder A** and drop it on the 'Orion' diskette, the file will be located both in **Folder A** and on the diskette (the file has been copied).

In other words, when you transfer a file to another storage medium you copy it.

The file is now stored in **Folder A** and on the diskette.

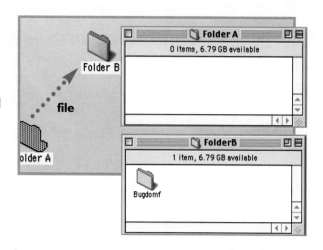

Aliases (see point 7 on the previous page)

An alias provides fast access to a file from several places on the disk without your having to duplicate the file. An alias has the same name as the file, but the characters '(alias)' are added.

The icon of the alias is the same as that of the file, except that a small up-arrow is added and the file-name is in italics. You can delete the alias word from the file name if you wish.

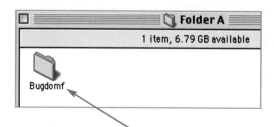

The file now remains in folder **A** but is also saved on the Orion diskette (it was copied, not moved).

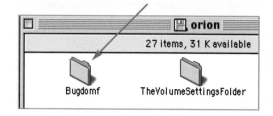

The Trash can

The *Trash can* is used for two things: to store files you intend to delete, and to eject an external disk such as a diskette, Zip, CD-audio or DVD. Bear in mind that files placed in the *Trash can* are not really deleted, but are kept there in case you need them again. To get rid of them permanently, you must empty the *Trash*.

Trash

The Trash can is full.

Trash

The Trash can is empty.

1. Removing files permanently

To remove a file permanently:

1 Put the file in the *Trash can*.

2 From the *Finder* menu, click *Special* and then *Empty Trash*.

3 The computer will ask you to confirm your request.

Special	Help
Empty Trash...	
Eject	⌘E
Erase Disk...	
Sleep	
Restart	
Shut Down	

⚠ The Trash contains 122 items, which use 67.2 MB of disk space. Are you sure you want to remove these items permanently?

[Cancel]   [OK]

4 To stop the warning message appearing in future, select the Trash can icon, press Command + I and untick the "Warn before emptying" box.

2. Stubborn files

You will at times come across files that simply refuse to be deleted. These are:

1 Files in use

2 Locked files

To delete a file currently in use, first close the file (sometimes you will need to close the application as well). To delete a locked file, first unlock it.

3. Unlocking a file

To unlock a file, select it and use the shortcut *Command + I* and untick the *Locked* box.

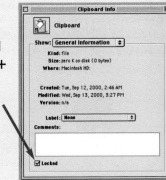

Clipboard Info

Clipboard

Show: General Information

Kind: file
Size: zero K on disk (0 bytes)
Where: Macintosh HD:

Created: Tue, Sep 12, 2000, 2:46 AM
Modified: Wed, Sep 13, 2000, 3:27 PM
Version: n/a

Label: None
Comments:

☑ Locked

Command + ← puts the currently selected item(s) in the Trash can.

4. Removing an external drive from the Desktop

The *Trash can* is also used to remove an external drive from the Desktop (such as a drive for a diskette, disk or **CD-ROM**). To do so, drag its icon to the *Trash can*. **MAC OS** can easily tell the difference between a file to be deleted and a disk to be removed, so you needn't worry about the operating system erasing the contents of a diskette.

The operating system will also refuse to remove a drive when certain items on it are still in use, and will inform you accordingly. If so, you may have to quit the relevant application and/or stop using a particular font.

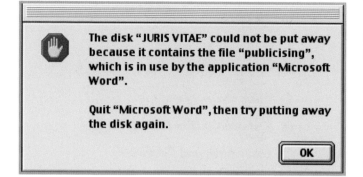

> The disk "JURIS VITAE" could not be put away because it contains the file "publicising", which is in use by the application "Microsoft Word".
>
> Quit "Microsoft Word", then try putting away the disk again.
>
> OK

5. Retrieving a file from the Trash

Sometimes you may send a file to the *Trash* by mistake. As long as the *Trash* has not been emptied, you can always restore it:

1 Double-click the *Trash can* icon.

2 Select the file you want to retrieve.

3 Move it out of the *Trash* (drag and drop).

Better yet:

1 Double-click the *Trash can* icon.

2 Select the file you want to retrieve.

3 Click the *File* menu.

4 Select *Put Away*: the file will be returned to its original location.

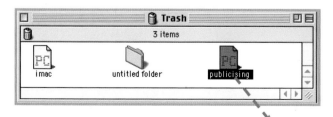

Move the file out of the *Trash*.

The same applies to folders. So you can send a folder to the Trash can and, as long as the Trash has not been emptied, retrieve it whenever you want, with two to three clicks of the mouse.

Setting the system date and time

One of the first things you should do is set the right date and time, so that you can manage your files, including e-mails, properly. This will enable you to search for a file by the date on which it was created or modified, and remove the risk that your correspondents who sort their e-mails by date might not notice your e-mail.

Setting your iMac's clock

1 Click the *Apple* menu.

2 Choose *Control Panels*.

3 Click *Date and Time*.

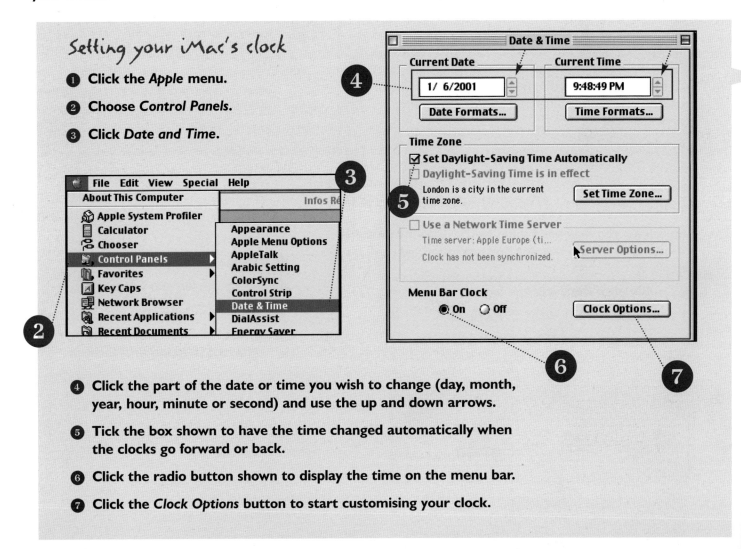

4 Click the part of the date or time you wish to change (day, month, year, hour, minute or second) and use the up and down arrows.

5 Tick the box shown to have the time changed automatically when the clocks go forward or back.

6 Click the radio button shown to display the time on the menu bar.

7 Click the *Clock Options* button to start customising your clock.

Displaying the time and chiming

1 Tick the option boxes as you wish to customise your clock and have it chime on the hour.

2 You can also choose your favourite chime.

Clock Options

Menu Bar Display Format
- ☑ Display the time with seconds
- ☑ Append AM/PM to the time
- ☑ Show the day of the week
- ☐ Flash the time separators
- ☐ Show the battery level
- ☐ Use custom clock color:

Select Color...

Sample

Thu 12:34:56 PM

Chime Settings
- ☑ Chime on the hour
  - ☐ ...number of times as current hour
  - ☐ ...unless a screen saver is running

Select Chimes
- ⏲ SimpleBeep ⬍
- 🕐 Laugh ⬍
- 🕐 Logjam ⬍
- 🕐 Temple ⬍

Font Settings
Font: Charcoal ⬍
Size: 12 ⬍

Cancel   OK

Set Time Zone

Select the closest city in your current time zone:

City	Country
Brussels	Belgium
Bucharest	Romania
Budapest	Hungary
Buenos Aires	Argentina
Cairo	Egypt
Calcutta	India

Cancel   OK

Note

If you have an iBook, set the time zone as well. Then all you have to do when you travel is to change the time zone, and your clock will change automatically to local time.

Finding files and folders

The iMac's operating system has included a highly sophisticated search utility called *Sherlock* from the outset (since the first version). MAC OS 9, the latest version of the operating system, features an updated version of *Sherlock* (version 2).

Sherlock 2 is a search program for both the iMac and the Internet. Here we'll focus exclusively on the iMac environment (hard disk, diskettes, etc.), and deal with the Internet later.

First you must index the contents of your iMac. This operation may take from a few minutes to several hours, depending on the quantity of data on your computer, so it's best to schedule it for when you're not using your iMac (at night, for instance).

1. Indexing

This operation consists of creating a file (an index) containing all the important words on your disk drive.
As you'll find out, the size of the index file increases with every indexing operation. To create an index, type *Command + L* and select the drive you want indexed; then click *Index* or *Update*, depending on whether the drive has already been indexed.

If you want to schedule the indexing operation at a given time, click the *Use Schedule* box, then click *Schedule* and enter a schedule that suits you.

You can easily verify that a volume has been indexed.

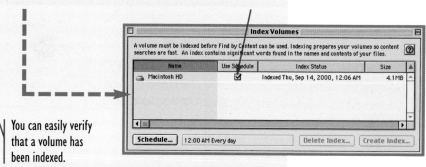

2. Finding by file name

❶ Click the hard-disk icon.

❷ Enter a word or phrase that is part of the name of the file you want to find.

❸ Select the *File Names* radio button.

❹ Click the magnifying-glass button.

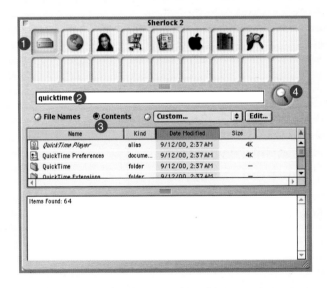

3. Finding by content

❶ Click the hard-disk icon.

❷ Enter the word or phrase you want *Sherlock* to find within the files on your hard disk. Remember that this type of search can be carried out only if the hard disk has been indexed.

❸ Select the *Contents* radio button.

❹ Click the magnifying-glass button.

4. Conduct a custom search

1 **Click the hard-disk icon.**

2 **Enter the word or phrase to describe your custom search (for example, 'pictures').**

3 **Select the *Custom* radio button (other options appear when you click the scroll arrows).**

4 **Click *Custom*. The screen will display a window (see next page) with dozens of options to help you customise your search as precisely as you want.**

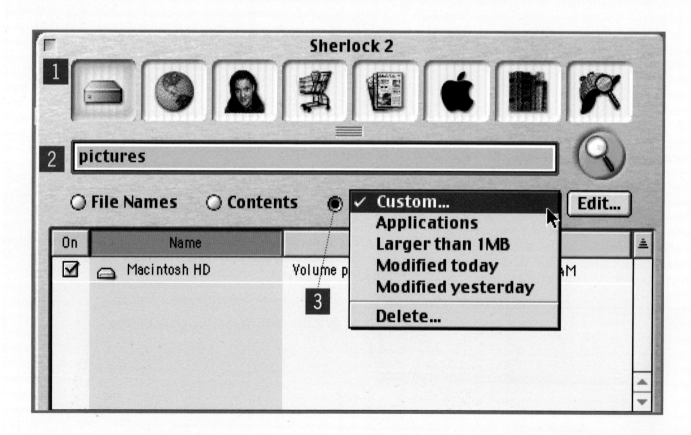

To find out exactly where any file is that *Sherlock* finds, click its name and a second window will show the folder hierarchy.

The items found are shown in the first window. Each column button can be used to sort in a new order. For example, you can sort by *Size* or by *Kind*. If you perform a *Content* search, a *Relevance* column appears.

Display by Relevance.

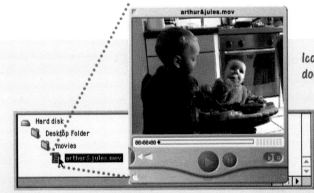

Icons in the windows are normal icons; double-click an icon to open its item.

Help

Help is available whatever you're doing with your iMac (which does not necessarily mean that you will always find the information you want). The search engine serves up some strange answers sometimes, and you may need to look through every page of the results because the search criteria are not always strictly adhered to.

Help
Help Center
Show Balloons
Mac Help   ⌘?

To get help :

❶ Go to *Finder*.

❷ Click the *Help* menu.

❸ Three options are displayed:

   ⓐ *Help Center*
   ⓑ *Show (Hide) Balloons*
   ⓒ *Mac Help*

1. Show Balloons

When you select this option, the operating system will display help balloons each time the cursor lingers on an object for a few seconds. Though interesting at first, these balloons will begin to get on your nerves when you've mastered the basics of the operating system. When that happens, simply select this option again to remove them.

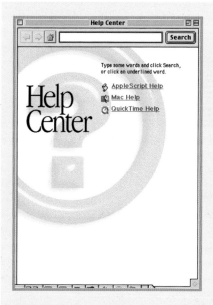

2. Help Center

You can conduct two types of search in the *Help Center*:

❶ By topic (click on one of the topics listed)

❷ By keyword

Searching by keyword

Enter the keyword (for example, 'shortcut') and click the *Search* button. The results of the search are displayed in order of relevance, as shown in the example opposite.

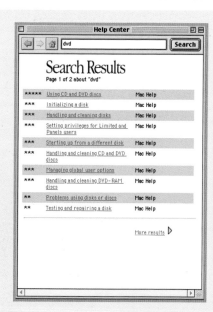

3. Mac Help

The screen layout is the same as that of the *Help Center*, but now information is arranged by lists of topics.
For example, *What's new* groups all the topics concerning the new features of Mac OS 9.0.

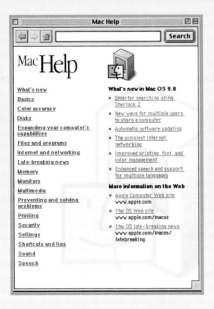

One way to get help is to hold down the Ctrl key and click the object for which you want help. In the drop-down menu that will appear, click Help.

4. Assisted Help

Some topics obtained through the *Help Center* contain small assistants that help you carry out the desired operation.

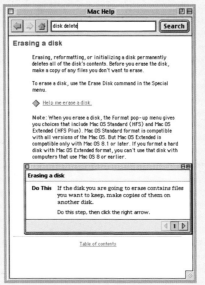

Take, for example, the module *Erasing a disk*: the system carries out the command to erase a disk step by step with you. Until you've carried out each required operation, you won't be able to go to the next stage...

Search tips

To refine your search, you can use the following special boolean characters:

Function	Character
AND	+
OR	|
NOT	!
GROUP	( )

To obtain the character, click Alt + Shift + I.

Keyboard shortcuts

A keyboard shortcut consists of two or more keys pressed in combination to carry out a certain operation. This is often faster than having to open menus and select the appropriate option, and will spare you having to use the mouse.

Edit	View	Specia
Undo		⌘Z
Cut		⌘X
Copy		**⌘C**
Paste		⌘V
Clear		
Select All		**⌘A**
Show Clipboard		
Preferences...		

There are so many keyboard shortcuts, not only for general operation of your iMac but also for various programs, that it's impossible to remember them all. Here are some basic ones you should memorise, however, as they'll get you out of many a bind.

In brief

There are two advantages to keyboard shortcuts:

1. They are faster than using the mouse and drop-down menus.
2. They can perform operations that cannot be carried out with the mouse alone.

A keyboard shortcut for a menu option is usually indicated in the menu alongside the option itself.

> The *Option* key is also known as the *Alt* key.

---

1. Keyboard shortcuts to start the computer

To start the computer	Press	
Boot from CD	C	
Disable extensions	Shift	
Rebuild your Desktop	Command + Option	
Re-initialise the PRAM	Command + Option + P + R (hold down the keys until you hear the starting tone a second time).	

2. Basic shortcut keys

To	Press	
Quit a program	Command + Q	
Create an alias	Command + M	
Put a file away	Command + Y	
Create a new file	Command + N	
Open a new file	Command + O	
Print	Command + P	
Find	Command + F	
Search on the Internet	Command + H	
Select all	Command + A	
Cancel	Command + Z	
Copy	Command + C	
Paste	Command + V	
Cut	Command + X	

3. Keyboard shortcuts to unfreeze a frozen program or the computer itself

To	Press	
Power-on the computer	**The power button**	
Quit a frozen application	**Command + Option + Esc**	
Soft shutdown	**Command + Option + Shift + Power Button**	
Soft restart	**Command + Control + Power Button**	

Notes

• You may need to rebuild your Desktop if certain information displayed on it is damaged (for example, if the program icons are no longer displayed).

• The PRAM (parameter memory) is a small section of memory containing information about your system's settings. It's a good idea to reinitialise this memory if the computer starts acting erratically – the initial values will then be restored. The disadvantage of such re-initialisation is that certain settings (mouse, video card, sound, type-ahead buffer, etc.) have to be restored manually. You do this from the Control Panels (see page 33). Reinitialisation requires a keen ear. If you don't hear the restarting tone a second time, the PRAM has not been reinitialised, most probably because you were holding down the Shift key.

Warning

All unsaved work will be lost when you quit a frozen application or computer.

Chapter IV

Mastering your iMac

Changing the appearance of your Desktop

If you don't like the way your Desktop looks, you can easily change its appearance.

A. Hide the Control Strip

You can reduce or extend the *Control Strip* by dragging its tab, and you can add items to it.

You can hide the strip as follows:

1. Open the *Apple* menu.
2. Click *Control Panels*.
3. Click *Control Strip*.
4. Select *Hide Control Strip*.

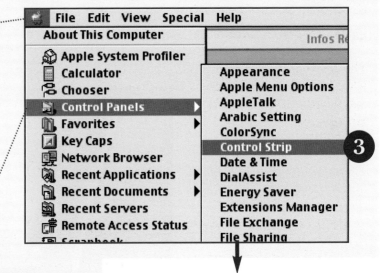

You can use the tab to reduce or extend the Control Strip.

B. Using your own Desktop picture

You can use your own desktop picture instead of the ones supplied. Save it as a **JPEG** file at a resolution of 72 pixels per inch. The image will need to be 800 x 600 pixels if you want it to fit neatly on the iMac screen.

Then open the *Appearance* control panel and go to *Desktop/Place Picture* (or *Remove* the current picture if necessary). Locate the picture on your hard disk and click *Set Desktop*.

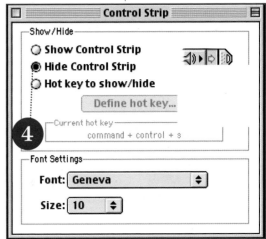

C. Customise your Desktop

① **Open the *Apple* menu.**

② **Choose *Control Panels*.**

③ **Select *Appearance*.**

The program will display a very full window containing six tabs. Select each tab in turn and make the desired changes.

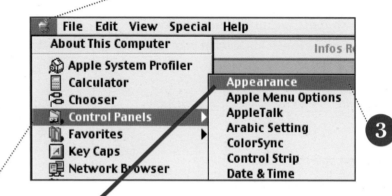

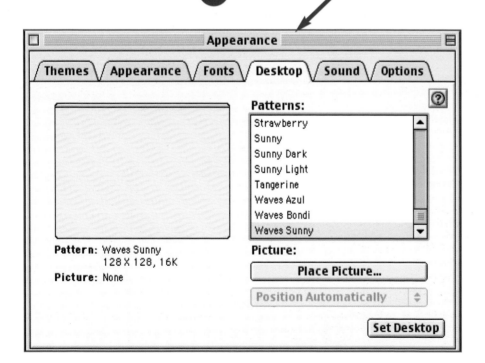

Installing new character fonts

The iMac is delivered with an impressive set of fonts; however, you may wish to use other fonts to give your documents a more personal touch. Although some fonts are very expensive, you can buy **CD-ROMs** teeming with fonts for just a few pounds.

To be able to use these fonts with your programs, you must first install them. Once a font is installed, it can be used by all your applications.

Installing fonts

1. Open the hard disk.

2. Find the *System Folder*.

3. Select the fonts you wish to install (from a diskette, for example).

4. Drag the fonts to the *System Folder*.

5. The iMac will display a message to the effect that the fonts must be stored in the *Fonts* folder (a subfolder of the *System Folder*).

6. Click *OK*.

However, if you have a 'font suitcase' application such as *Adobe Type Manager Deluxe* or *Symantec Suitcase*, you can store your extra fonts anywhere on your hard disk without dragging them into the *System Folder*.

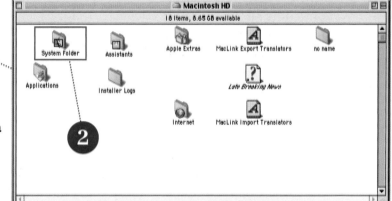

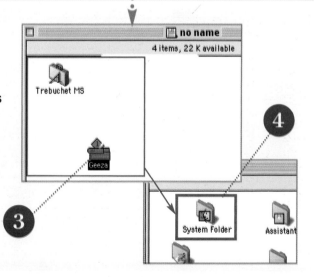

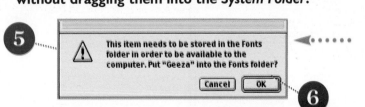

Viewing fonts

1. **Open the *Apple* menu.**

2. **Select *Key Caps*.**

3. **In the new menu, select *Fonts*.**

4. **Open the menu and select a font.**

5. **Press the keys on the keyboard to view the characters available with this font.**

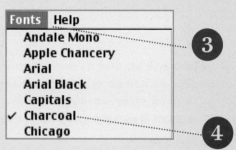

Notes

• To gain access to a new font from an application that is already running, you must first close it and then reopen it.

• The fonts have different icons, depending on their type and origin.

Mastering the Extensions Manager

Extensions are small programs that enhance the possibilities of the operating system. Your iMac is delivered with a core set of extensions that are managed by an executive program called *Extensions Manager*. These factory-installed extensions will almost never cause any problem for the iMac. Other extensions you install (often without being aware of doing so) each time you add a new program or a new driver to your iMac may cause conflicts.

Symptoms of extension conflicts

These symptoms will appear as soon as you power-on the computer or launch certain programs or, for no apparent reason, after working for a few minutes or hours. The most frequent symptoms are:

» **Your iMac freezes.**

» **A dialogue box with a coded error message appears.**

» **A program doesn't work, although it worked fine the day before.**

» **Your iMac crashes.**

Understanding how the Extensions Manager works

We shall see that there are several ways of dealing with these problems, but first it's important to understand how the *Extensions Manager* works.

To access the *Extensions Manager*:

❶ **Click the *Apple* menu.**

❷ **Choose *Control Panels*.**

❸ **Select *Extensions Manager*.**

❹ **The program updates its database.**

❺ **The screen displays the extensions panel (after a few seconds and maybe with a warning screen).**

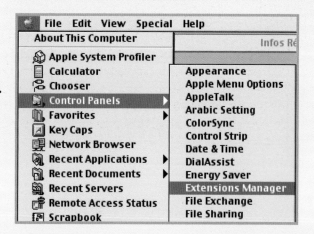

The extensions panel is divided into three parts:

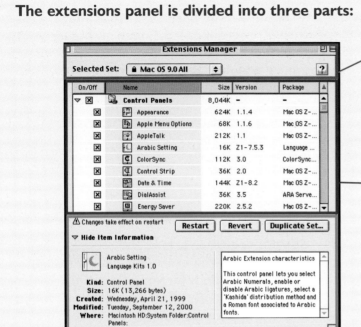

❶ **The first part displays the selected set. You can choose several types of configuration using the scroll-bar: base set, complete set, customised set, etc.**

❷ **The second part displays an impressive list of extensions indicating, for each extension, the:**
- **Status (on/off)**
- **Name**
- **Size**
- **Version**
- **Package**

❸ **The third part is used to obtain information about each extension. When you select an extension, the lower part of the table provides not only all the technical information concerning that extension, but also a brief description of what it does and how it does it. The date an extension was created is very important, because old extensions can cause problems when you install a new operating system (such as the Mac OS 9, for example). So you should replace old extensions by their more recent versions, which you can usually find on the Web.**

If an extension conflict occurs:

A. Save the current set:

❶ Click the *Duplicate Set* button.

Duplicate Set...

❷ Give a name to this set.

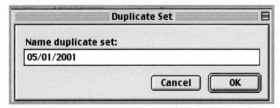

B. Go back to the factory-installed set:

❶ Open the *Set* menu

❷ Select *Mac OS 9.0 All*.

❸ Click *Restart*.

The computer should now restart without any problem, exactly as it did on the first day (for it now has the very same extensions as on that first day). The only problem is that new extensions which were needed for new peripheral devices and programs are no longer loaded. So this is only a temporary solution, and you must now find out which extension was causing the problem.

Isolating an extension conflict

To isolate the conflict, you must return to the set that was causing the problem. You can always try to isolate the troublesome extension manually, by ticking and unticking the active extensions one by one until you find the extension causing the problem.

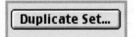

But this operation is long and tedious. So if you cannot isolate the extension conflict rapidly, use a program to do it for you. One of the best such programs is *Conflict Catcher*, which will find not only the application causing the problem but also the solution to that problem (usually, changing the order in which extensions are installed will do the trick).

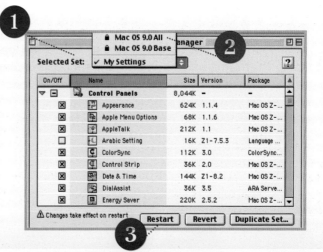

Deactivating an extension temporarily

You may also wish to deactivate an extension because it causes problems, takes up too much disk space or is rarely used.

☒	Item is on
☐	Item is off
⊟	Folder contains some items that are off and some that are on

All you have to do is to tick the small box in front of its name (see opposite).

You will have to restart the computer for the new changes to take effect.

If the computer refuses to start because of an extension conflict:

1. Power the computer on and hold down the *Space bar* until the *Extensions Manager* panel appears.
2. In *Select Set*, choose *Mac OS 9.0 All*.
3. Click *Restart*.
4. The computer will restart, keeping only the original extensions.

If this process fails, try dragging potentially troublesome extensions out of the system altogether. As a last resort, reinstall the original system software.

Note

Without extensions the operating system is very limited. For instance, you will not be able to print, play audio CDs or read PC diskettes on your iMac. Pay close attention to what is happening on the screen, because you could inadvertently format a diskette.

Starting without extensions

You may wish to start the computer without any extension for a variety of reasons, such as:

- You need to use the computer for an urgent job (and have no time to deal with extension conflicts).

- You want to make sure that the problem is caused by extensions and not by something else.

The simplest thing to do is to start the computer while holding down the *Shift* key; no extension will be loaded (and the welcome screen will inform you accordingly).

Multiple users

With Mac OS 9, you can customise access to your iMac for up to 40 people. In this way, you can limit the rights of certain users in order to maintain a certain level of data confidentiality and to restrict access to certain peripherals. Each user will thus have a more or less extended personal environment.

1. Preparing the computer

Before you program your computer for multiple users, you must first give it a network identity:

❶ Click *Control Panels*.

❷ Choose *File Sharing*.

❸ Enter a name for the computer (e.g. the owner's name).

❹ Enter a password.

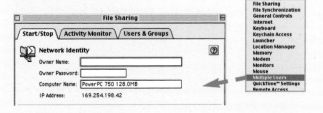

2. Types of user

Mac OS recognises four kinds of user:

❶ **Owner**: Has all rights.

❷ **Normal**: Has most rights, but may not access documents of other users.

❸ **Limited**: Has limited rights (depending on the access boxes ticked).

❹ **Panels**: Has even more limited rights (the authorised programs appear in a panel and the documents authorised for use with that program in another panel).

Normal user.

Limited user.

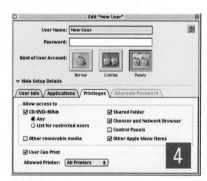

Panels user.

3. Creating a user account

To create a new user account:

1. Open the *Control Panel* and select *Multiple Users*.
2. Click *New User*.
3. Enter the name and password of the new user.
4. Select the kind of user.
5. Click *Show Setup Details*.
6. Select a *User Picture*.
7. Click the *Applications* tab and tick the appropriate boxes and radio buttons.
8. Click the *Privileges* tab and tick the appropriate boxes and radio buttons.
9. If you wish to create a voice password, click the *Alternate Password* tab.
10. Tick the other boxes according to the kind of user.
11. Click the *Close* box to confirm.

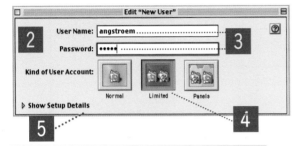

Note

Step 8 is for the selection of programs and step 10 for the selection of peripherals (CD, printer, etc.)

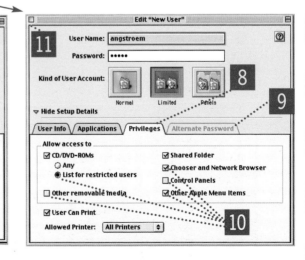

Using the Clipboard, Stickies and Scrapbook

The *Clipboard*, *Stickies* and *Scrapbook* are three utilities for storing information (such as texts, images and sounds). Information is stored temporarily on the *Clipboard*, but information stored on the *Stickies* and *Scrapbook* can be kept for years.

A. The Clipboard

The *Clipboard* contains information you have stored using the *Finder*. To copy information, for example, you select the section that interests you in the application's window and press *Ctrl + C*. You can then paste information from the *Clipboard* into other applications by pressing *Ctrl + V*.

To view the contents of your *Clipboard* at any time:

❶ Click *Edit*.

❷ Select *Show Clipboard*.

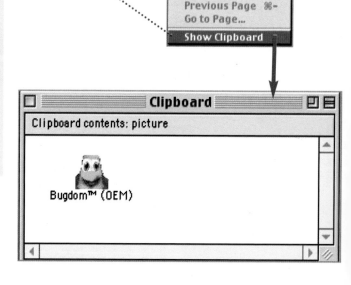

Note

The item contained in the Clipboard will be replaced when a new Copy or Cut operation is carried out, and cleared when you switch off your iMac.

B. Stickies

Stickies is used to write small notes and stick them to your Desktop, where they can serve as reminders.

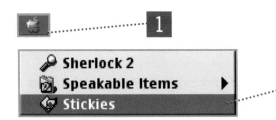

I. To run *Stickies*:

❶ Click the *Apple* menu.

❷ Select *Stickies*.

WELCOME TO STICKIES!

Stickies lets you write notes (like these) and stick them to your screen. You can use Stickies to jot quick notes, to write reminders, or to store frequently used text. Your notes are visible whenever the Stickies program is active.

Stickies automatically saves your notes. You don't have to choose "Save" or choose a place to save your notes. Stickies does it for you.

2. To create a note:

❶ Click *File*.

❷ Select *New Note*.

I love you

A few notes...

Notes

• You can stick as many notes to your Desktop as you wish.

• You can create notes in different colours to make them easier to distinguish.

• Each note has a close box, a zoom box, a size box and a title bar.

3. To display your notes in the foreground when you start your iMac:

Open the application, then in the menu bar:

❶ Click *Edit*.

❷ Choose *Preferences*.

❸ Tick *Launch at system startup*.

❹ Untick *...in the background*.

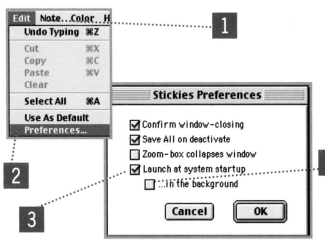

4. Processing notes

Your notes can be imported, exported, saved, printed, etc.
Saved notes are stored on the hard disk as *SimpleText* **by default.**

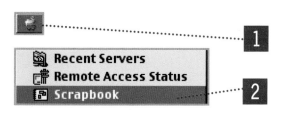

I. To access the *Scrapbook*:

❶ **Click the** *Apple* **menu.**

❷ **Select** *Scrapbook*.

2. To store an item in your *Scrapbook*:

❶ **Drag the item's icon to the** *Scrapbook*;
or

❷ **Copy the contents of the** *Clipboard* **using** *Edit / Paste (Command + V)*.

3. To send an item from the *Scrapbook* to an application:

❶ **Copy the item using** *Edit / Copy (Command + C)*.

❷ **Paste the item into the application with** *Edit / Paste (Command + V)*.

C. The Scrapbook

You can use the *Scrapbook* **to store all kinds of documents you use frequently, such as text, images, sounds, video and even 3D objects. The** *Scrapbook* **has been part and parcel of the Macintosh since the first Mac Plus!**

4. 3D objects

3D objects can be viewed from every angle, using the mouse and the positioning icons.

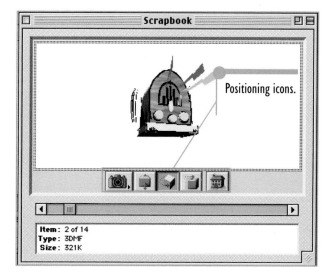

TIP
You can move around the Scrapbook using the scroll-box arrows.

Creating an automatic summary

Your iMac can create an automatic (albeit not always convincing) summary from any text.

1 Create a text with your usual word processing program.

2 Copy this text to the Clipboard (Command + C).

3 Open the Clipboard (Edit menu/Show Clipboard)

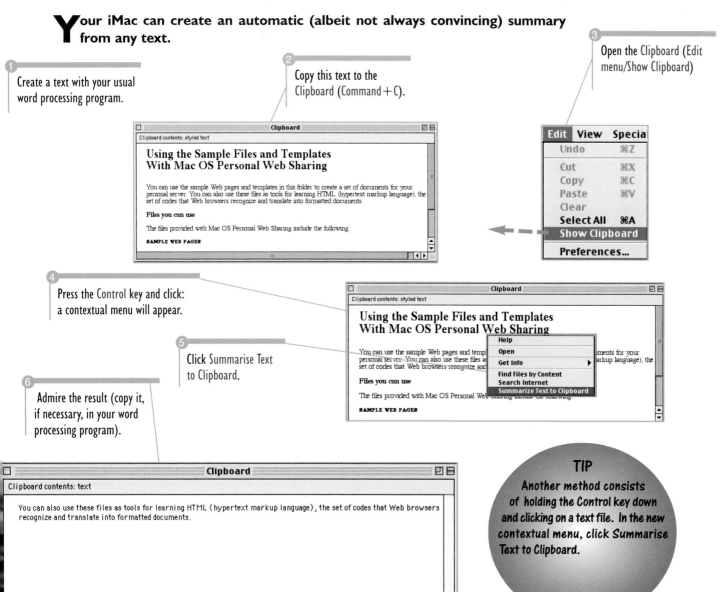

4 Press the Control key and click: a contextual menu will appear.

5 Click Summarise Text to Clipboard.

6 Admire the result (copy it, if necessary, in your word processing program).

TIP
Another method consists of holding the Control key down and clicking on a text file. In the new contextual menu, click Summarise Text to Clipboard.

Managing your memory

The iMac manages different types of memory:

- **RAM**
- **PRAM**
- **Cache**
- **Virtual Memory**
- **Memory allocated to programs**

RAM

This is the central memory of your iMac. To find out the size of your computer's memory, go to *Finder*, click the *Apple* menu and select *About Your Computer*.

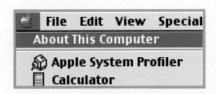

A. Types of memory

PRAM

PRAM is a small section of **RAM** memory used to store information about your system's settings (date, time, preferences, etc.) (see page 66).

Cache

The Cache is a reserved section of **RAM** for storing frequently used information. This memory can be set from the *Memory Manager*.

Virtual memory

This is an area of the hard disk that can be used as if it were **RAM**, when the system requires more **RAM** than is actually installed. The amount of disk space allocated to virtual memory can be programmed from the *Control Panels* (*Memory* option).

CHAPTER IV : MASTERING YOUR IMAC

Memory allocated to programs

This is the memory that a program uses to process its files. The amount of memory allocated for this can also be changed manually (see page 84).

...

B. Accessing the Memory Manager

To access the *Memory Manager*:

1 Click the *Apple* menu.

2 Select *Control Panels*.

3 Click *Memory*.

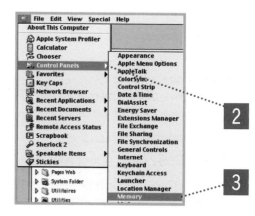

Cache memory

The settings of this memory can accelerate or slow down the performance of your computer. It all depends on how you use it. If the computer slows down, return to the default setting.

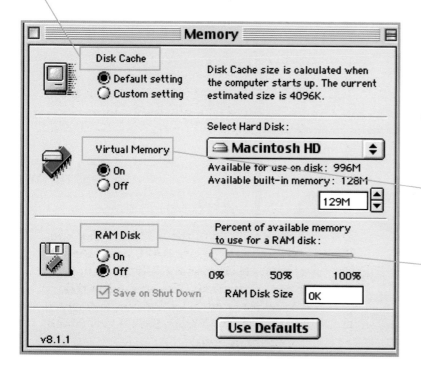

Virtual memory

The On radio button is usually selected, in which case part of your hard disk (to be specified) can be used as RAM. You'll have to deactivate the virtual memory (select Off) if you want to run certain video programs, in which case you must restart the computer for this change to take effect.

Virtual disk

Here a section of RAM is used as the equivalent of a fast disk. This memory is usually deactivated (selected Off), but can prove useful if you frequently use a diskette (whose contents you can place on the virtual disk) or in order to save energy when using your iBook (using diskettes frequently consumes a great deal of battery power).

Allocating more memory to a program

A program may sometimes inform you that it does not have enough memory to run the operation you want, especially when you're working with large files such as videos or full-colour images in **Adobe Photoshop**. If this is the case, you'll need to allocate more memory to the program.

Let's take the example of *Photoshop*, which often requires a lot of memory to process images.

1. Select the program (click the program icon, not an alias icon).
2. Type *Command + I*.
3. In the *Show* field, select *Memory*.
4. In *Preferred Size*, enter a larger value.
5. Tick *Locked*.

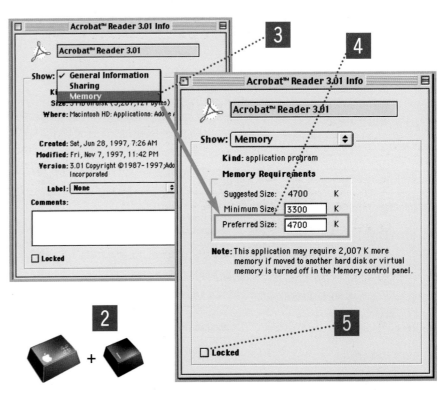

Note

To change the size of the memory allocated to an application, you must first quit that application.

Encrypting

If you want some of the documents stored on your hard disk to remain confidential, you can encrypt them using the Apple *File Security* utility.

This program performs three tasks:
- It creates a passphrase.
- It encrypts the document.
- It compresses the data.

You can encrypt files to keep on your hard disk, but you can also send encrypted files by e-mail (in which case you must communicate the passphrase to your correspondents).

1. Encrypting files

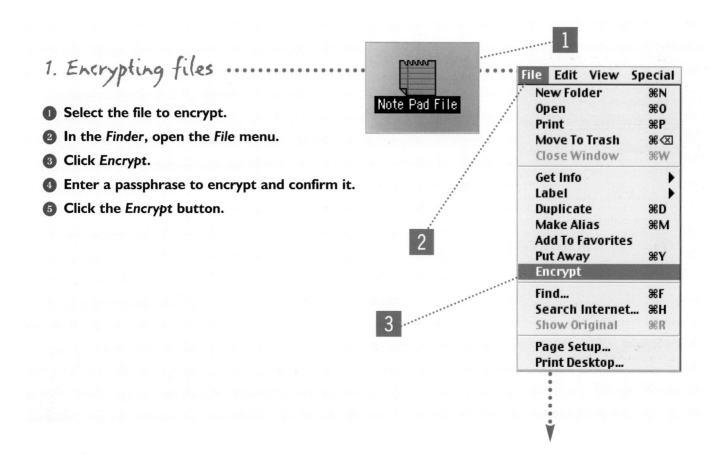

1 Select the file to encrypt.

2 In the *Finder*, open the *File* menu.

3 Click *Encrypt*.

4 Enter a passphrase to encrypt and confirm it.

5 Click the *Encrypt* button.

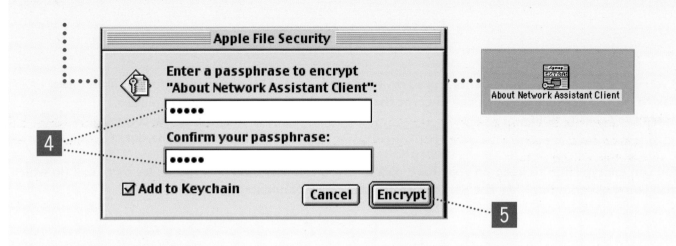

2. Decrypting files

1. Select the file to decrypt.
2. Double-click this file.
3. In the new screen, enter the passphrase.
4. Click the *Decrypt* button.
5. The file is opened.

If you wish to protect this file again, you must re-encrypt it.

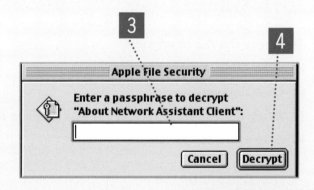

Note

This program cannot encrypt closed or locked files. So if the file is open, close it; if locked, unlock it.

You cannot encrypt:
- Folders
- Disks
- Volumes
- System folder items

TIP
If you already have an access keychain (see page 87), an additional screen will be generated when encrypting and decrypting to validate your key.

Keychain Access:
You'll never forget your passwords again

The keychain is a kind of safe where you can automatically save and keep all your access codes and passwords. If you create a keychain, you'll have only one password to remember. Your keychain will remember all the others.

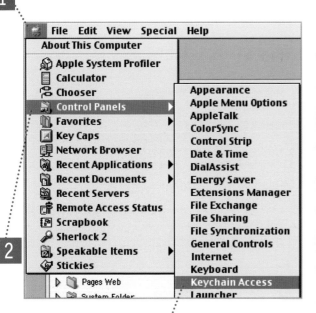

1. To create a keychain:

❶ Click the *File* menu.

❷ Select *Control Panels*.

❸ Choose *Keychain Access*.

❹ Click *File*, then *New Keychain (Command + N)*.

❺ Enter the *Keychain Name*.

❻ Enter the password and confirm.

❼ Click *Create*.

In order to be accessible, the content of your Keychain has to be unlocked by entering your password.

Note
If you have programmed your computer for multiple users (see page 76), each user already has a keychain.

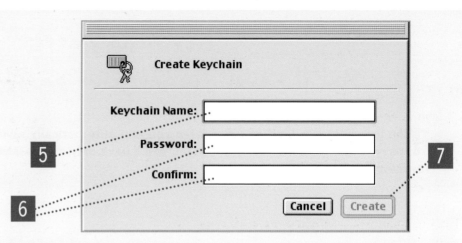

2. Locking and unlocking a keychain

A. Unlocked

When unlocked, the keychain shows the list of codes.

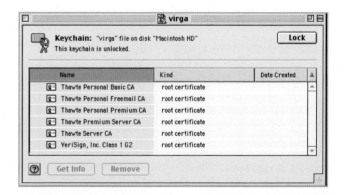

B. Locked

When locked, it shows only the *Unlock* button. You can lock a keychain on request (by clicking the *Lock* button) but also, as a precaution, after a period of inactivity or as soon as you leave your computer. To be safe, always lock your keychain when you aren't in front of your iMac.

3. Programming automatic locking

① Click the *Edit* menu.

② Select *Settings*.

③ Enter the password and click the *View* button.

④ Tick as indicated below.

⑤ Click *Save*.

The keychain will be locked after 10 minutes of inactivity.

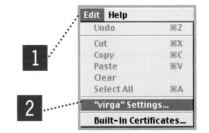

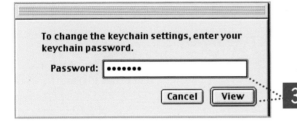

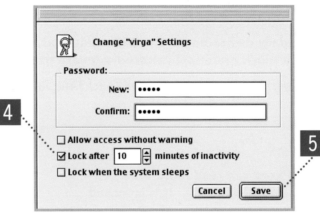

4. Adding items to the keychain

① Open the keychain.

② Create an Internet file for the address of a site (see page 128).

③ Drag this file to the keychain window.

④ The program will ask you to specify the information that it requires before it will allow you to access the site (identifier, password, etc.).

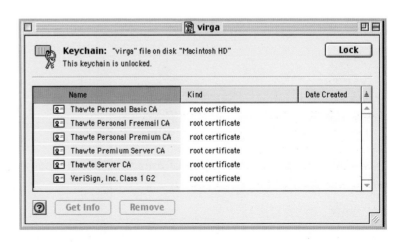

Discovering QuickTime 4

QuickTime is Apple's software designed especially for multimedia activities, and is also available for the **PC**. *QuickTime* reads most audio, graphic, video and animation formats on **CD-ROMs** and on the Web (in the latter case, a plug-in is needed to enable the browser – Explorer or Netscape – to read the format). Furthermore, many software applications have been adapted to read *QuickTime* formats. The software applications listed below can read *QuickTime* formats on the iMac:

- The browsers installed (Microsoft *Explorer* and Netscape *Navigator*)

- *SimpleText* (initially dedicated purely to handling text, *SimpleText* has since become a much more sophisticated software package)

- *QuickTime Player* (the specific player for *QuickTime* formats)

1. QuickTime Player

The *QuickTime Player* can read more than 200 different formats, including MP3. It is launched automatically whenever a multimedia file is opened, but you can also open it manually. All *QuickTime* extensions (and there are many) are placed in the *QuickTime* extensions file.

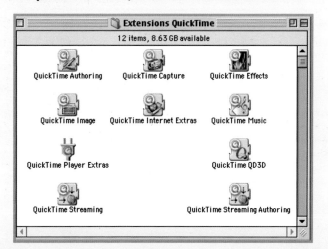

To run the *QuickTime Player*, double-click its icon.

QuickTime Player

Notes

- Mac OS 9.0 installs SimpleText in the Applications folder.

SimpleText

- Your browser can read QuickTime formats on the Internet if:

  - Its extensions are installed in the system folder;

  - The QuickTime plug-in is installed in the browser's list of plug-ins;

  - The connection settings are programmed in QuickTime Player.

QuickTime Player has an absolutely intuitive interface, as shown in the illustration below:

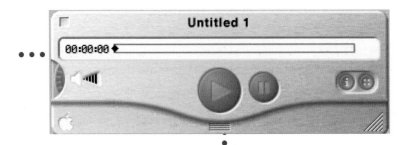

The wheel is used to adjust the volume.

The Play button launches the application (irrespective of the format of the data).

The i button provides information (when available).

This button drops down the control panel (fast forward, balance, bass, treble, etc.).

To view the table of video clips available on the Web, drag the pane using the mouse.

2. Reading QuickTime files on the Web

To read *QuickTime* files available on the Web, you must first set the connection speed:

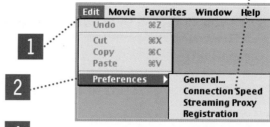

① **Click the *Edit* menu.**

② **Select *Preferences*.**

③ **Select *Connection Speed*.**

④ **Select the button for your type of connection.**

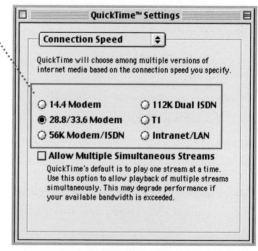

The *QuickTime* menu bar features many setting options, most of which we shall ignore for now. Worth mentioning here are *Auto-Play*, which automatically launches the program's CD player as soon as a CD is inserted in the drive, and *QuickTime Exchange*, which automatically converts a file so that *QuickTime* can play it.

3. Recording audio CD files

QuickTime allows you to record sequences from audio files:

① Insert an audio CD into the CD/DVD drive.

② Click *File* / *Open*.

③ Select a track.

④ Click the *Convert* button.

⑤ Click the *Options* button.

⑥ Click *Play* (to start recording), then later *Stop* (to stop recording).

⑦ Click *OK*.

⑧ Select a recording folder.

⑨ Name your file.

⑩ Click *Save*.

⑪ The file is imported: when the importing operation has been finished, a sound file (AIFF) will have been created on the disk.

Note

You must deactivate all the automatic sounds of your iMac (such as hourly chimes) while recording; otherwise, they will be recorded along with the music track.

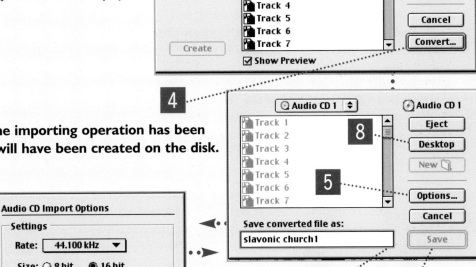

slavonic church1

4. TV portal

QuickTime is supplied with a number of links to **QuickTime TV**, Apple's TV portal. To access the **TV** portal's stations, drop down the pad under the buttons, and click one of the sites on offer (**BBC World, WB Records, Fox News,** etc.). You'll be connected to the Internet and, after a few seconds (remember, patience is a virtue!), the selected **TV** programme (specially designed for broadcasting on the Internet) will appear on your computer.

It doesn't amount to much at the moment, but it does give an inkling of what **TV** and the computer will be able to do together in future.

5. QuickTime Pro

The *QuickTime* version installed in your iMac is play-only. If you want to create applications in *QuickTime* format yourself, you'll have to register with **Apple** and pay a fee to obtain a registration code, which will turn your *QuickTime* program into the *Pro* version.
To find out more about *QuickTime*, visit the **Apple** site, which is regularly updated and features demonstrations and links to other sites dealing with *QuickTime*:

http://www.apple.com/quicktime

You can also check for updates and reach the Web site devoted to *QuickTime* from the *Help* menu.

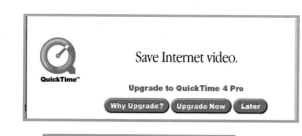

Chapter V

The peripherals

Connecting a peripheral to the iMac

To make the most of your iMac, you will have to connect a few peripherals. The list of available peripherals is extremely long, all the more so as the iMac has numerous ports for that purpose (Ethernet, USB, FireWire, AirPort, Video, headset, telephone, microphone and speaker). Many users, however, will not take advantage of every such port.

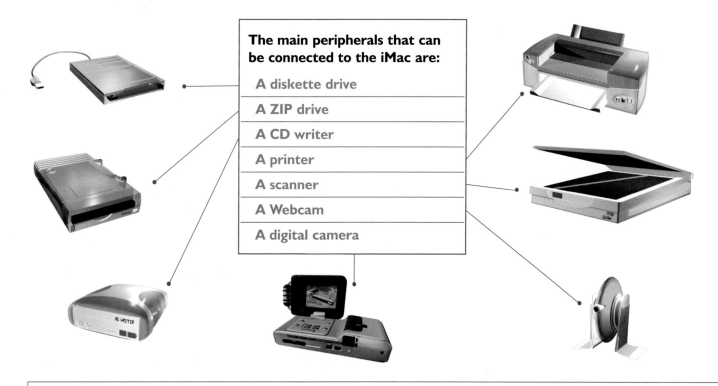

The main peripherals that can be connected to the iMac are:

A **diskette** drive
A **ZIP** drive
A **CD** writer
A **printer**
A **scanner**
A **Webcam**
A **digital camera**

Most recent peripherals have a **USB** output and can be connected to the **USB** port, which will unquestionably be the most widely used port on the iMac. In many cases, however, the number of USB ports available is simply not enough, and you'll have to use what is known as a hub. Our next section will be devoted entirely to the **USB** port and how it is used; here, we shall first take stock of the main iMac peripherals.

Brief reminder about the iMac's ports

USB	**All types of recent peripherals.**
Ethernet	**Printer, network.**
FireWire	**Digital still camera, digital movie camera, hard disk, CD writer.**
Video	**External monitor.**

1. Diskette drive

This is the first peripheral you should connect to the iMac if you want to keep track of your documents and transmit them without using the Internet. The diskette drive is connected to the USB port and is not delivered with an external power supply (which is why it cannot be connected to the keyboard's USB port).

If you connect to the keyboard, you risk getting the following message:

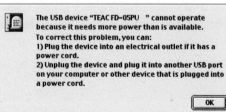

The USB device "TEAC FD-05PU   " cannot operate because it needs more power than is available.
To correct this problem, you can:
1) Plug the device into an electrical outlet if it has a power cord.
2) Unplug the device and plug it into another USB port on your computer or other device that is plugged into a power cord.

OK

2. ZIP drive

This storage medium is much appreciated by users who transfer large files between computers. A Zip drive can contain up to 100MB or 250MB of data, depending on the model. A Zip drive with a USB port can be connected to both the iMac and the PC.

3. CD writer

This peripheral allows you to store up to 650 MB on a single disk. This makes it ideal for amateur photographers and video makers. You can also use it to create your own music compilations for a pound or two (the price of a recordable CD). CD writers are distinguished by their reading/writing speeds, usually given as a multiple of normal real-time playing speed: 2X, 4X, 8X etc. The fastest CD writers use the FireWire port, but most of them are connected to the USB port (or to the hub, to be more precise).

4. Scanner

A scanner is used to scan photographs into digital-image form. They can then be edited using an image retouching application, or placed on your Web page. You can also use a scanner for optical character reading, i.e. to digitise printed text into a character stream that can be read by a word processor. If your scanner has a transparency hood, you can scan transparencies too.

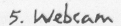

5. Webcam

A Webcam is a small camera (connected to the USB port) used to send a continuous stream of images across the Web. It can also be used for continuous surveillance (for example, of a child's bedroom or a waiting room) and to organise videoconferences on the Internet – a minimal investment for considerable enjoyment.

6. Digital still camera

This camera can be connected to the **USB** or the **FireWire** port. Film-based cameras, where you have no further control of a photograph once you've taken it, are becoming things of the past. Now you can correct your photographs, embellish them, give them more glamour or more drama, etc., even ten years later. High-end digital still cameras have sensors with more than 3,000,000 pixels and allow enlargements up to 20 x 25 cm format.

7. Digital movie camera

This camera is connected to the **FireWire** port. The iMac is delivered with *iMovie* software, which enables you to make perfectly edited short films (images, text and sound) in a matter of hours. The latest versions of the iMac DV are delivered with *iMovie 2*, which is even more sophisticated.

8. Printer

The printer, together with the disk drive, is unquestionably the most useful peripheral and deserves a chapter on its own.

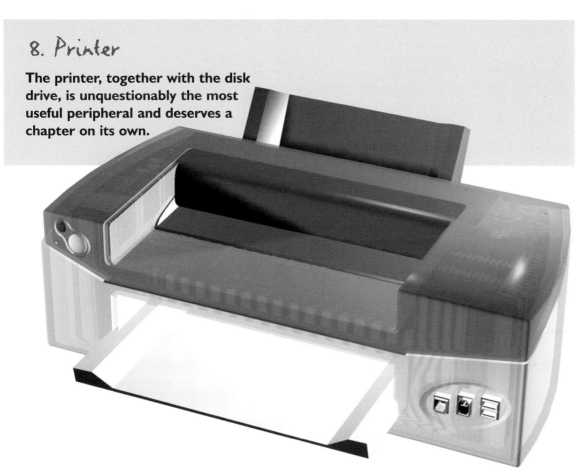

Using adapters to connect your old SCSI peripherals
You may still have peripherals that use SCSI technology rather than USB. You can connect them to your iMac, but you will need an adapter that is compatible with the particular make of peripheral you want to connect. Check on the adapter manufacturer's Web site for a list of compatible peripherals. You may also need to download a new software driver from the peripheral manufacturer's Web site.

You can print with any printer on any type of paper, but obviously with widely varying results. An inkjet printer is the most suitable for the widest variety of printing tasks. It can even be used to print colour photographs, provided you use the right paper for that purpose. The most common types of paper are:

Standard paper

Used for printing texts. Photos printed on this type of paper will be of poor quality (dull, with de-saturated colours, smudges, spills etc.) because the ink soaks into and mixes uncontrollably with the fibres in the paper.

Special inkjet paper

Bright white coated paper, used to print graphics and photos because smudges and spills are minimal and the colours are more vibrant and less saturated than with standard paper.

Photo paper

Richly coated glossy paper for a real photographic look and feel. This paper is specially designed to control ink absorption and to provide vibrant colours without smudges or spills. It is used only to print photographs.

USB ports and hubs

Your iMac has only two **USB** ports. To connect the numerous **USB** peripherals your computer probably needs (keyboard, mouse, disk drive, scanner, Zip drive, etc.), you'll need a hub.

A hub is a common connection point containing multiple ports. **We'll use the keyboard and mouse connection to explain how a hub works.**

When you installed your iMac, you connected the keyboard output to one of your computer's USB ports and discovered that you could plug the mouse into one of the keyboard's USB ports (on the right or on the left, depending on whether you are right-handed or left-handed).

The keyboard acts as a hub, because it contains two ports but takes up only one of the computer's ports.

These ports can be used only by peripherals that have their own power supply or that consume minimal power. Therefore, you cannot connect a diskette drive (which has no external power supply) to one of these ports, because the power for the drive would have to be supplied directly by the **USB** port.

Terminology

There are several varieties of hub, and it's worth taking the time to understand the differences between them.

Self-powered hubs

These are powered from an electric outlet. A self-powered hub contains 4 to 7 USB ports.

Bus-powered hubs

These are powered from the computer's bus, without any external power supply. The keyboard is essentially a bus-powered hub. Only a peripheral that consumes little power (such as a joystick or a mouse) can be connected to it, and certainly not one that acts as a hub (so it is out of the question to connect two keyboards together).

Which hub should you buy?

So you'll need a hub in order to connect a disk drive, a printer and a **CD** writer to your iMac. The hub is connected to the iMac's free port at one end (the other port is used for the keyboard), and to the power supply at the other. It contains 5 to 7 connectors for peripherals. Remember that each cable must be shorter than 5 metres (otherwise, you'll have to create a cluster structure with another hub).

Advantages of a USB peripheral

1. Plug and play (the device is recognised as soon as it is connected). If the driver is missing, the system will ask for your permission to download it automatically from the Internet.

2. Hot swapping (the device can be connected or disconnected while the computer is on).

3. No identification or termination number (as was the case with the earlier SCSI technology where a number had to be assigned to each device).

4. Up to 127 self-powered peripherals can be chained.

5. High data-transfer rate (up to about 1 MB/sec).

For more information, go to
www.apple.com/usb

Printing

Information technology has not yet ushered in the paperless age; on the contrary, it would appear that we have never printed so much. The printer is the computer's basic peripheral – all the more so because you often have to print pages found on the Internet (it's not so easy to jot down the contents of a page from the screen and then file it!).

Today, users can choose between two types of (affordable) printer:

- **Colour inkjet.**
- **Monochrome laser.**

Laser printer

Laser printers are fast and inexpensive to use. They are ideal if you want to print a lot of text.
If you'll be using your printer for professional applications such as layout, you should opt for one with PostScript capacity, even if the price is slightly higher. Laser printers can be connected to the Ethernet port or, more rarely, to the USB port.

PostScript

PostScript is a page description language (PDL) that is indispensable for most desktop publishing (DTP) tasks, but is not available on most inkjet and low-end laser printers.

Inkjet printer

There are an impressive variety of
inkjet printers on the market. If you
can afford it, you should buy a photo-
realistic printer (so that you can print
high-quality digital photos) with two ink
cartridges, one black and one colour.
Inkjet printers are not expensive to buy,
but they are expensive to use. Their
cartridges, despite being expensive,
have a limited printing capacity. Inkjet
printers are usually connected to the
USB port.

1. Getting started with your printer

To print a document, you must:

1 Connect a printer to the iMac.

2 Select the printer in a selection panel. *Chooser* is the important
menu for managing printers – the one you use to install your
default printer or to change printers if necessary. To open this
menu:

3 Click the *Apple* menu.

4 Select *Chooser*. ....

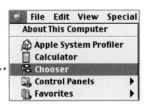

The following menu will open:

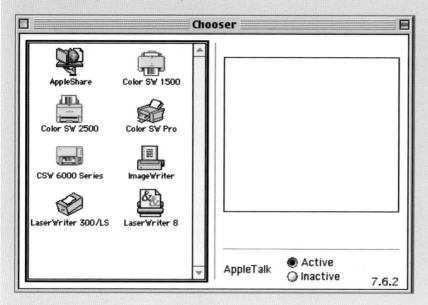

Some Apple printers are already included in this menu by default. Other printers will be listed once they are installed (from the **CD-ROMs** delivered with the printers).
The procedure will differ depending on whether you already have a printer or whether you're installing one for the first time.

A. Connecting a new USB inkjet printer

1 If this is your first printer, it will necessarily have a **USB** connection. The physical installation will therefore consist of connecting the printer to the free **USB** port, then installing the required drivers from the **CD-ROM** delivered with the printer. Once you've followed all the steps, the installation program will ask you to restart the computer.

2 Open the *Chooser* as described above, and click your printer's icon.

3 Select the **USB** port and click *Setup*.

4 Click the *Chooser* window's close button.

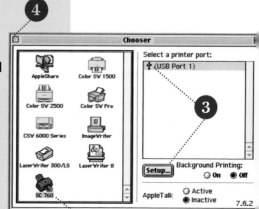

B. Connecting an old printer

If you already have a printer with a serial or parallel port, connecting it will be a little more complicated, because the iMac has neither a serial nor a parallel port. Luckily, manufacturers now offer adapters for three types of connectivity:

- . **USB to parallel.**
- . **USB to serial.**
- . **Ethernet to serial (*LocalTalk*).**

USB to parallel

This adapter is used to connect a parallel printer to a **USB** port. The HP Printer Cable kit for a **USB** Mac can be used on most Hewlett-Packard inkjet or laser printers.

Notes

• You can also connect a printer to the Fire-Wire port or through the AirPort wireless network, but these options are still rarely used.

• You may need to download updated driver software from your printer manufacturer's Web site

USB to serial

Several kits are available on the market: they are used to connect scanners, digital cameras and some inkjet printers through the **USB** port. It's worth noting that this type of kit does not recognise *LocalTalk* printers (i.e. most of the laser printers designed for the Macintosh), nor all inkjet printers. You should therefore find out whether the kit you are thinking of buying is compatible with your peripheral.

Ethernet to serial (*LocalTalk*)

Asanté makes a small package that is placed between the iMac's Ethernet port and the serial port of a laser printer. As the connection is made via *LocalTalk*, this package can be used to connect all laser printers, including older models.

2. Choosing (installing) a printer

Once the physical connection has been established, you can install your printer. The procedure will depend on whether you are choosing a **PostScript** or a **non-PostScript** printer.

A. Non-PostScript printer (connected directly to the computer)

1. Open the *Apple* menu.
2. Select *Chooser*.
3. In the new window, click on the type of printer connected to your computer.
4. If necessary, the program will display a new screen in which you must click *Create/Settings* and follow the instructions that appear.
5. Click the *Chooser*'s close button.

C. PostScript printer

Here you must have a printing service that will be created automatically. This printing service will appear on your Desktop as an icon with the name of the selected printer. Click on this icon and Mac OS will open a window allowing you to manage the printing operation.

LaserJet 4

B. Non-postscript printer (Networked)

1. Open the *Apple* menu.
2. Select *Chooser*.
3. In the new window, click on the type of printer connected to your computer.
4. In the appropriate window, select a printer name.
5. If necessary, the program will display a new screen in which you must click *Create/Settings* and follow the instructions that appear on the screen.
6. Click the *Chooser*'s close button.

AppleTalk

AppleTalk was the local area network architecture built into the first Macs. Even when the computer was not networked, an **AppleTalk** port was necessary for connecting most laser printers. Today, the iMac no longer has an **AppleTalk** port, but if you have an old laser printer and connect it by an **AppleTalk** cable to the Ethernet port, you should be able to use it.

1. Open the *Apple* menu.
2. Select *Control Panels*.
3. Select *AppleTalk*.
4. In the *Edit* menu, click *User Mode*.
5. Select *Administration*.
6. Click the *OK* button.
7. In the *Connection* menu, select *Ethernet*.

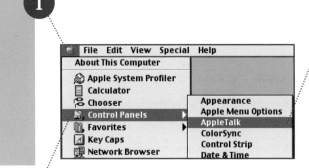

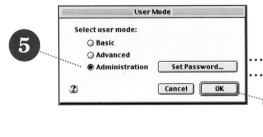

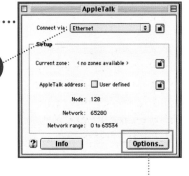

Note

To activate or deactivate the AppleTalk port, click the Options button. In fact, this is the only correct way to activate or deactivate this port (do not use the Chooser).

Built-in peripherals

A built-in peripheral may sound a paradoxical term, but it's justified, because a peripheral is a device literally 'peripheral' to the heart of the computer proper (the central processing unit or CPU).

The iMac has four built-in peripherals:

- The monitor.
- The modem.
- The CD-ROM (DVD) drive.
- The speakers.

1. The monitor

The monitor is built into the central processing unit, and can be easily set up in the Apple menu:

1 Open the *Apple* menu.

2 Select *Control Panels*.

3 Select *Monitors*.

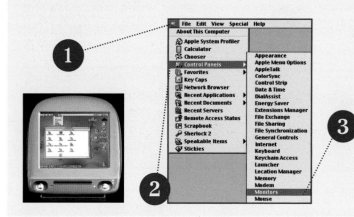

The program displays the screen below in which you can change the main settings.

The effect of clicking each option will be shown directly on the screen.

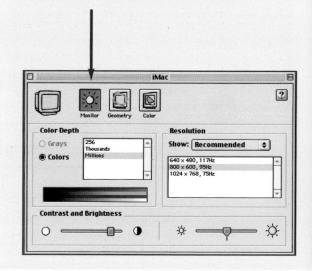

Note

Some iMacs have a door at the back for accessing a VGA connector. You can plug a larger monitor than the iMac's into it and thus take advantage of the highest resolution of the iMac card (1024 x 768). This new monitor will display an image identical to that on the iMac screen.

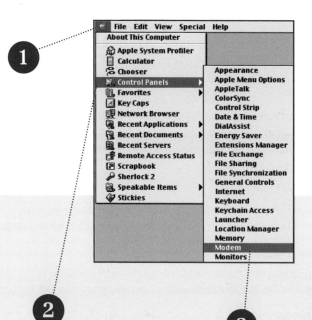

2. The modem

The iMac uses the latest generation of modem technology for its built-in modem, which you can adjust from the *Modem* menu:

1 Open the *Apple* menu.

2 Select *Control Panels*.

3 Select *Modem*.

The program will display the screen below in which you can change the main settings.

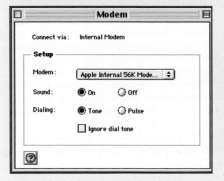

The modem is used to connect to the Internet in different ways, but most often via the telephone. All you have to do is to connect the telephone input of the modem (on the right side of the iMac) to the telephone outlet in your home.

The latest iMacs also feature a new wireless transmission technology called *AirPort* (see next page). This technology is still quite expensive, however, and its advantages are rather limited.

AirPort

AirPort is an Apple utility that manages wireless data transmission to constitute a network (for networked games, for instance) and a connection to the Internet. AirPort replaces the infrared port of the first iMacs. As already mentioned, however, it is still quite expensive.

To use the wireless transmission feature, you will need:

1. A specific card called an AirPort Card.   2. An AirPort base station.   3. An aerial (antenna – already built into your iMac).

AirPort Card

This small card must be inserted in the slot for that purpose at the base of the iMac.
It has a maximum range of 45 metres and can transmit data at up to 11 megabits per second.

AirPort base station

This communicates with the AirPort Card. So you must connect it to the network, to the telephone line or to the cable modem, depending on which one you use.

Installing the card

The card is very simple to install. You simply insert it into the appropriate slot (which you can open using a coin) and connect the aerial wire to it.

AirPort base station.

3. The CD-ROM (DVD) drive

Audio CDs

Your iMac can play all audio CDs with excellent sound quality, as the new iMac models have high-quality speakers.

 As soon as you insert an audio CD, your iMac will launch the CD player as a background task.

Audio CD controlling

To control the audio CD, you must run the *Apple CD* application. Double-click an audio track icon. The CD player will be displayed – as you can see opposite, the control panel is very similar to that of conventional CD players.

In brief

If you have a CD writer, you can use your iMac to make audio CD compilations for private use.

4. Using the DVD player

Some iMacs (the DV series) have a **DVD drive** instead of a **CD-ROM** drive. This can play audio disks and CD-ROMs, of course, but also DVD disks. No iBook has this peripheral built in yet.

A. To play a DVD disk

1 Insert the **DVD** disk into the drive.

2 Click the *Apple DVD* player.

3 The screen will now display:
    The film contained on the disk, shown in the viewer
    The DVD player controller
    A menu bar

B. The controller

You can show or hide the controller from the menu bar. Just click on 'Window', Show/Hide controller.

C. The menu bar

It packs all the features we can expect from a DVD player, including:

- **Choice of soundtrack language**
- **Choice of subtitles**
- **Parental control**
- **Freeze frame**
- **Skip section**

Notes

• The viewer and the controller can be moved just like any other window. The menu bar is hidden in certain cases. To show it again, move the cursor to the bottom of the screen.

• By selecting half-size (Video / Half-size) you can continue to work on your iMac and watch a video at the same time (you will, of course, need to be able to multi-task yourself to do so...).

Chapter VI

The Internet

Configuring your iMac for Internet access

The iMac has been optimised for the Internet (as its name implies and the absence of a removable disk drive confirms). To access the Internet, your computer will need a certain amount of information about you and about your service provider. Fortunately, all this information can be handled in a single control panel, and the various programs you use will access it directly from there.

There are several ways to configure your iMac for Internet access. The most common (which will work on all computers) is the following:

❶ Click the *Apple* menu.

❷ Select *Control Panels*.

❸ Click *Internet*.

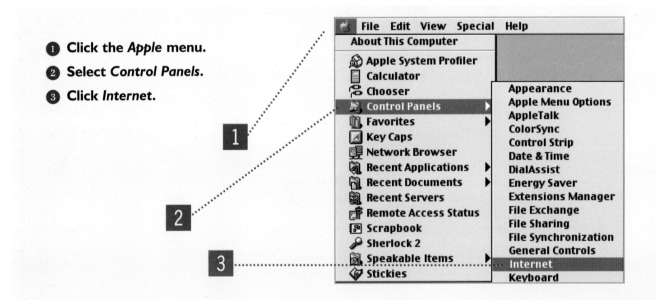

Note

Many service providers nowadays distribute free CD-ROMs that will automatically install onto your hard disk all the programs needed for the Internet. Microsoft Internet Explorer (and more rarely Netscape Navigator) and Outlook (an e-mail application) are usually included. This procedure is fine if this is your first connection or if you are familiar with the intricacies of the programs provided. It is not recommended in other cases, however, because you will find it extremely difficult to restore your initial settings.

The operating system opens a window that includes 4 tabs.

1. Personal

Enter your name and the e-mail address provided by your service provider (i.e. the company that provides your Internet access).

①

If you have several sets, select the set that must be active. The active set is that of your provider.

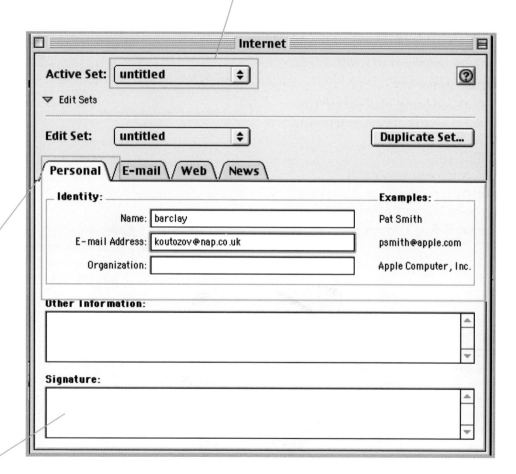

②

Click the Personal tab and enter values for the fields relating to your identity on the Internet.

③

Enter a text string or an ASCII 'drawing' to serve as your signature on all the messages you send across the Internet. This signature will be independent of any other signature you may enter for use by the e-mail software.

2. E-mail

Enter the e-mail account information provided by your service provider:

- **Your user account ID (or login or access code)**
- **Your incoming mail server (the name usually starts with POP)**
- **Your password**
- **Your outgoing mail server (the name nearly always starts with SMTP)**

Make sure you enter this information exactly as it appears on the document provided to you by your ISP.

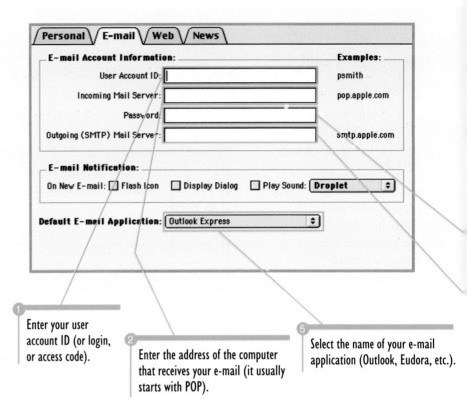

Enter your user account ID (or login, or access code).

Enter the address of the computer that receives your e-mail (it usually starts with POP).

Select the name of your e-mail application (Outlook, Eudora, etc.).

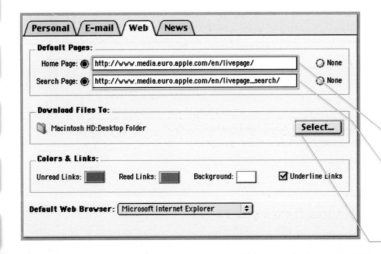

3. Web

You may well leave everything as is in this tab:

Enter the address of the Internet page that will be automatically loaded into your Web browser each time you log on.

Enter the Internet address of the default search engine that you want to use.

Select the folder in which you want to store files that you download from the Internet.

4. News

This tab concerns newsgroups. Leave the fields blank if you're not interested in newsgroups. Otherwise:

- **Enter the address of the news server proposed by your service provider, or:**
- **Enter the address of another news server.**

Enter the address of the news server you wish to use. This address is not necessarily that of your service provider's news server. There are many news servers, and some are more specialised than others in the range of newsgroups that they make available.

③ Enter the password given to you by your service provider.

Enter the address of the computer that sends your e-mail (its name usually starts with SMTP or relay).

| Personal | E-mail | Web | **News** |

News Server Settings:

News (NNTP) Server: `msnews.microsoft.com`

Connect to news server as: ○ Guest ⦿ Registered User

Name:

Password:

Examples:

nntp.apple.com

Default News Application: Outlook Express ⬍

E-mail address

An e-mail address is composed of two parts separated by the 'at' sign (@) . The first part is your identification (perhaps your first name and surname). The second is the address of your service provider or the organisation that has granted you an e-mail address (you can thus have several e-mail addresses for private and business use).

Examples: chrisbattersby@sweetershop.co.uk (business address)

ChrissieB@scottynet.com (private address)

ChrissieB@accordions.org (address used to exchange messages with members of a club)

Using the Internet Setup Assistant

Another very simple method is to use the *Internet Setup Assistant* and follow the steps shown on the screen. If the *Setup Assistant* is not on your Desktop, use *Sherlock* to find it and then double-click its icon.

The *Setup Assistant* will ask you simple questions and program your Internet access according to your replies. At the end, you can ask it to summarise everything to make sure you haven't made a mistake.

① **Internet Access.**

② **Do you already have an Internet account?**

Answer *No*, then click the various arrows until you get to Screen 5. Select a country, then a provider. The computer is now ready to connect to the site of the provider you have selected. To accept this connection, click the *Proceed* button.

All you have to do now is to answer the questions about your ISP.

Note

If you already have an Internet account, reply Yes to the question of step 2. Answer the various questions put to you afterwards, and in Screen 4 enter the telephone number you dial to connect to your service provider.

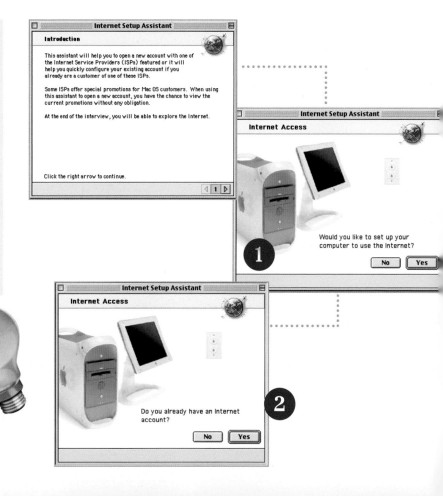

Launching and quitting an Internet connection

The two main reasons why people use the Internet are still to send and receive e-mail and to surf the Web. Mac OS 9 includes three programs for these activities: Outlook Express (an excellent e-mail and newsgroup manager), Microsoft Explorer (a browser) and Netscape Navigator (a complete suite comprising a browser, an e-mail manager, a newsgroup reader and other programs).

A. Launching an Internet connection

All you have to do is to start up an application designed for the Internet (such as a browser or an e-mail application) and your system will establish an Internet connection automatically. If this does not happen, proceed as in B and then click *Connect*.

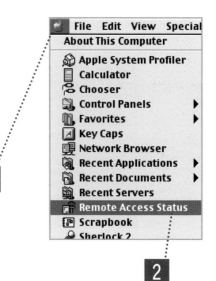

B. Quitting an Internet connection

1 Click the *Apple* menu.

2 Select *Remote Access Status*.

3 Click the *Connect/Disconnect* button.

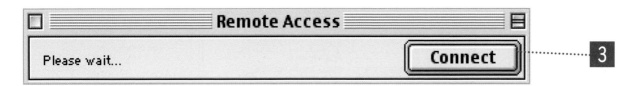

Useful menus and connection set-up

Although Apple's approach is intended to simplify matters, it's easy to get lost in the various menus concerning your Internet connection, and for once the PC approach is simpler. Here is a brief summary of some particularly useful items, all available from the *Apple* menu:

1. Remote Access Status

To disconnect from the Internet.

2. Internet

To configure your connection (service provider, e-mail address, password, newsgroups, etc.).

3. DialAssist

To set up your modem (useful for certain telephone lines and for long-distance calls and cards).

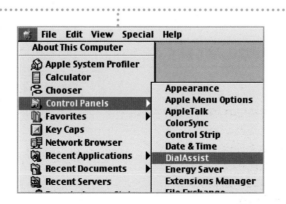

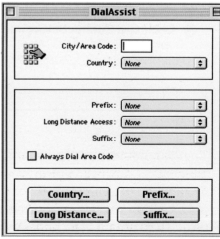

4. Modem

To program certain modem settings.

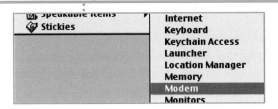

5. Remote Access

To set up a connection to the Internet.

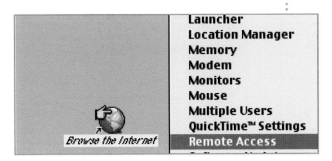

Setting up the connection

The *Remote Access* menu is used to program certain connection settings. For instance, you can arrange to disconnect automatically if your Internet link stays idle for a certain period, or you can be prompted every so often to maintain the connection (for absentminded users who think they're no longer on-line).

Warning!

Do not confuse Remote Access Status in the Apple menu (which is used to connect and disconnect) and Remote Access in the Control Panels menu (which is used to set up the connection).

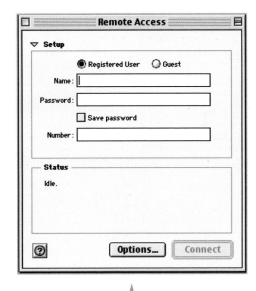

Searching on the Internet

Sherlock 2, iMac's search module (see page 58), can conduct very precise searches on the Internet. The basic program is configured for seven types of specific search (each referred to as a channel), but you can always create your own channels according to your personal criteria. The program will propose a choice of search sites for each channel. To select a search site, you simply tick its box. You'll note that each type of channel is presented differently. This illustrates that *Sherlock* is an intelligent search engine.

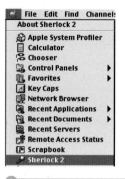

The original channels

Internet

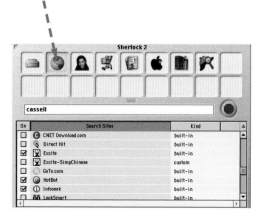

This channel displays a list of search engines. Tick the one(s) through which Sherlock is to conduct a search. The search engines can find everything that is indexed on the Internet. Each engine has its specific features, so it makes sense to use several search engines simultaneously.

People

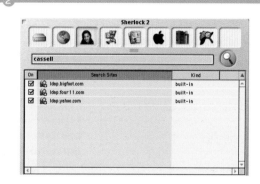

This channel displays a list of directory sites from which you can try to track down an individual or organisation. These special-purpose search sites use a process that is optimised to handle such directories. Tick the sites you are interested in. To make your search as effective as possible, it is best to use several such sites.

Shopping

Apple has selected a few shopping sites... but you can always add others.

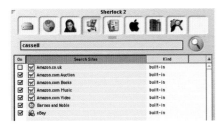

News

Apple has selected a few news sites... but it's up to you to see whether they're well suited to your interests and needs.

Apple

This channel provides information on Apple products. There are of course many other sites that you can discover for yourself

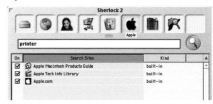

Reference

This shows a list of encyclopaedias, dictionaries and other reference sites, to which you can add sites that reflect your particular areas of interest.

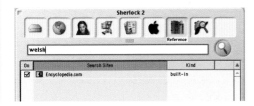

My Channel

This channel is empty. You can populate it with data from other channels by going to the Sherlock plug-ins site:
http://www.apple.com/sherlock/plugins.htm

The original channels can-not be changed or removed, even if you don't like them or find them insufficient. The only way to add items to your channels is to create channels yourself.

Automatic software update

One of the advantages of the Internet is that you can download software updates such as bug corrections and new drivers. The iMac has everything you need for such automatic updates:

> 1. At your request;
>
> 2. At time intervals that you specify.

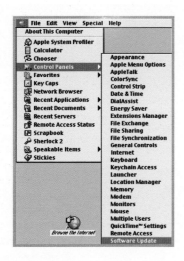

① Click the *Apple* menu.

② Select *Control Panels*.

③ Select *Software Update*.

A. Immediate update

① Click the *Update Now* button.

① The program connects to the Internet.

① The program downloads the updates.

B. Scheduled update

1 Tick *Update Software Automatically.*

2 Click *Set Schedule.*

3 Enter the time and date for the automatic update.

In addition to updating software applications, the operating system can also update your search channels on the Internet. Just go to Sherlock 2 (see page 124), empty a channel, then click its icon. You will receive the following message on your screen, and your computer will connect to the Internet.

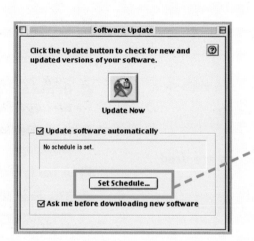

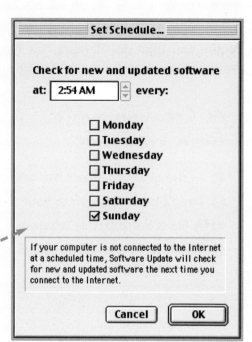

Note

If the computer is not switched on at the scheduled time or if it's not then possible to log on to the Internet, the program will remember your request and check for new and updated software next time you log on.

Creating aliases for the Internet

The easiest way to access a site more quickly or to send an e-mail immediately is to create a specific file for the site or for the address.

When you then double-click this file, you open the Internet application (browser, e-mail, etc.) and immediately access the address specified in the file.

A. Creating a file for a Web page

1. **In the browser, select the address of a Web site.**
2. **Drag this address on to your Desktop.**
3. **A file is immediately created.**
4. **The first 30 characters of the address are used to name the file.**

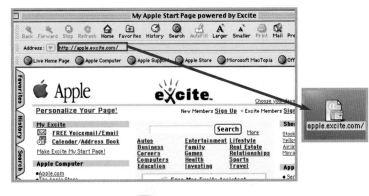

B. Creating a file for an e-mail address

1. **In the e-mail program, select a message from a correspondent.**
2. **Drag this message on to your Desktop.**
3. **A file is immediately created.**
4. **The first 30 characters of the message are used to name the file.**

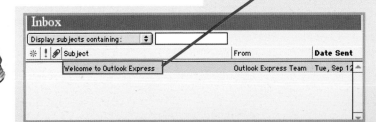

Note

Mac OS can create 8 different icons depending on the type of connection, such as for newsgroups or FTP (File Transfer Protocol).

Chapter VII

The iBook

The iBook

The iBook is the portable version of the iMac and is available in several versions. These differences have essentially to do with the colour of the computer and the processor speed (300 or 360 Mhz).

Everything already said about the iMac operating system also applies to the iBook. The main difference in using the two is the iBook's independence and portability, which is ensured by batteries that can function for 6 hours. So when you use your iBook on the road, take every precaution to minimise its power consumption – something you don't need to worry about if the iBook is plugged into the mains.

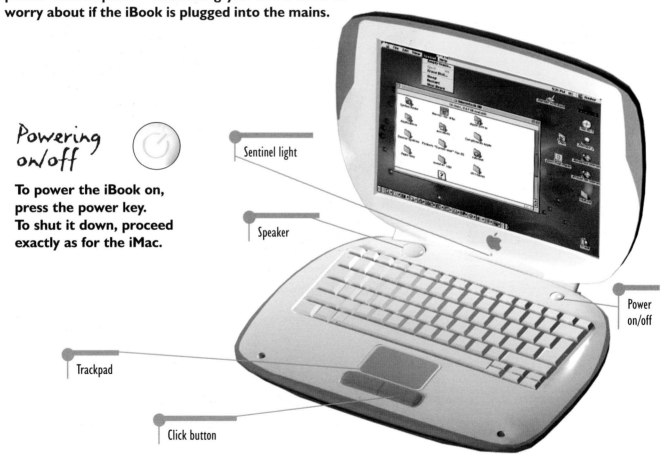

Powering on/off

To power the iBook on, press the power key. To shut it down, proceed exactly as for the iMac.

Sentinel light

Speaker

Power on/off

Trackpad

Click button

Interfacing

The interfacing on the iBook is less complete than on the iMac. However, there are 3 ports on the left of the keyboard:

• a modem port

• an Ethernet port

• a USB port

The iBook has the necessary interfacing for an external speaker.

The CD-ROM drive (there is no DVD drive) is located to the right of the keyboard, where the outlet for the mains adapter is also located.

The iBook can easily be dismantled if you want to install additional memory or an *AirPort* card. Since the components are quite delicate, however, we advise you to call on specialists for such operations.

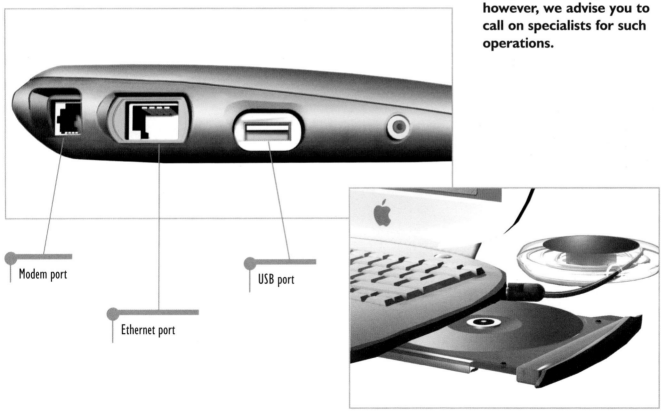

Modem port

USB port

Ethernet port

The trackpad

The iBook has no mouse, but you can, if you wish, plug one into the USB port, when it will function immediately.

With the iBook, you use the trackpad, a small area sensitive to the touch and movement of your finger, as you would ordinarily use a mouse. You'll get the hang of it after a few hours.

Trackpad click button

To set the trackpad:

1. Open the *Apple* menu.
2. Select *Control Panels*.
3. Select *Trackpad*.

The keyboard

Though necessarily reduced in size, the keyboard has everything!

In addition to the three standard function keys (*Ctrl*, *Alt* and *Command*), there is now a new function key (*fn*) etched in green. You use it to access the symbols etched in green on the keyboard (including all the numbers).

The function keys F1 to F12 are also available, but only the first six are already programmed:

The other function keys can be programmed as already explained (see page 36).

F1 and F2	Adjust the screen's brightness.
F3 and F4	Adjust the speaker's volume.
F5	Turn the ordinary keyboard into a numeric keypad (keys etched in green are now dedicated to numbers without having to use the fn key). It is the only key with a small indicator to show that it has been activated.
F6	Turn the speakers on or off (mute).

(see page 36).

The screen

The iBook has an active matrix screen that is very easy to read and is only slightly smaller than that of the iMac. It supports two resolutions: 640 x 480 and 800 x 600. As already explained, the screen settings can be changed by clicking the *Apple* menu, and then selecting *Control Panels / Monitors*. Unfortunately, no external monitor can be connected to an iBook (this, and the lack of a diskette drive, are the iBook's two real shortcomings).

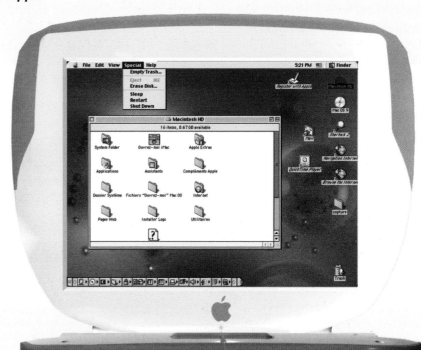

Indicator LEDs

1. The charge indicator **LED** (yellow when the battery is charging, green when it is fully charged) is situated at the mains adapter.

2. The idle-indicator **LED** (visible even when the iBook is closed) is green and blinks at regular intervals. It is located under the screen's Apple logo.

Battery functions

1. Checking the battery charge level

You can check the battery charge level on the *Control Strip*, where vertical lines indicate the battery level, the rate of discharge (which will enable you to see for yourself that some peripherals consume a great deal of energy) and the time remaining before you have to recharge the battery.

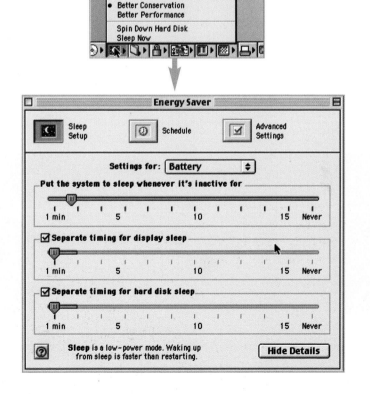

Time remaining.

2. Saving energy

In the *Control Strip*, click the moon icon, and select *Open Energy Saver Control Panel*. In the menu that appears, change the settings to save maximal energy but still allow you to work properly (there is no point putting your system to sleep every time it's inactive for a couple of minutes when you're completing a database where each item requires five minutes of search time).

Chapter VIII

Appendices

Calculators

The iMac – or its operating system, to be more precise – features two calculators: a conventional calculator and a graphing calculator. To make things easier, we'll move the graphing calculator from the *Applications Folder* (where it's usually kept) to the *Apple* menu.

A. Moving the graphing calculator to the Apple menu

1 **Open the hard disk.**

2 **Open the *Applications Folder* (and find the *Graphing Calculator* file).**

3 **Open the *System Folder* (and find the *Apple Menu Items Folder*).**

4 **Move the *Graphing Calculator File* to the *Apple Menu Items Folder*.**

5 **Close all folders.**

6 **Open the *Apple* menu: you should now have two calculators linked from it.**

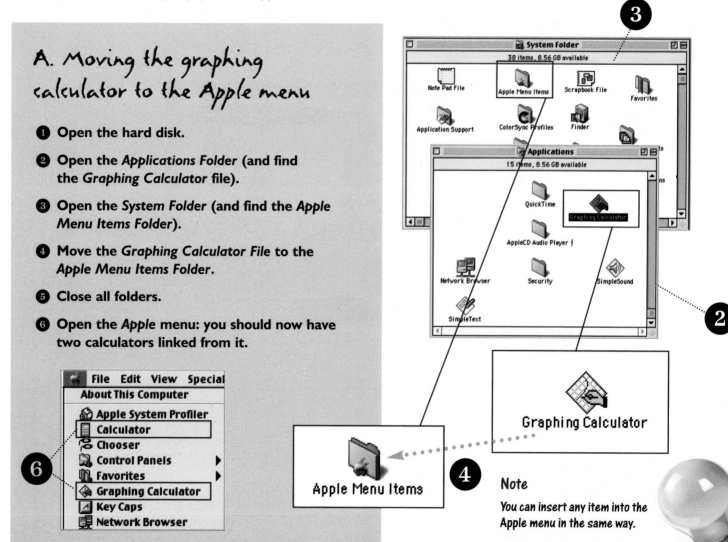

Note

You can insert any item into the Apple menu in the same way.

B. Using the calculator

① Open the *Apple* menu.

② Select *Calculator*.

You can now enter numbers and mathematical symbols either by using the mouse or from your keyboard.

You can copy the result into any application with *Copy* and *Paste* (*Command + C* then *Command + V*).

The calculator

Note

The graphing calculator has its own, very complete help program, which explains in detail how to plot curves from arithmetic or algebraic formulae.

C. Using the graphing calculator

① Open the *Apple* menu.

② Select *Graphing Calculator*.

With the graphing calculator you can plot numerous curves and graphic animations in 2D and 3D. To see what this calculator can do, run the *Full Demo* program.

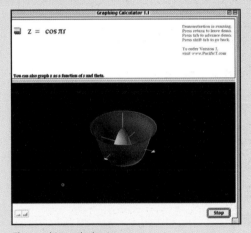

The graphing calculator

Installing other languages

Your iMac is capable of writing in Russian, Ukrainian, Bulgarian, Chinese, Japanese, Korean and Arabic – at no extra cost. When you consider how difficult it is to find a word processor in these languages, you might find it useful to know how to install the language kit delivered with the iMac. This kit is contained on the Mac OS 9 CD-ROM. The only thing you might have to buy if you use any of these languages frequently is a special keyboard.

> **To install the kit, you install in turn the:**
> - *Language Manager*   • fonts
> - **word processor**   • **keyboard**

A. Installing the Language Manager software

❶ **Open the Mac OS 9 CD-ROM.**

❷ **Open the *Software Installers* folder.**

❸ **Open the *Language Kits* folder.**

❹ **Click the *Install Language Kits* file.**

❺ **Check the languages you wish to install.**

❻ **Click the *Install* button.**

❼ **Restart the computer.**

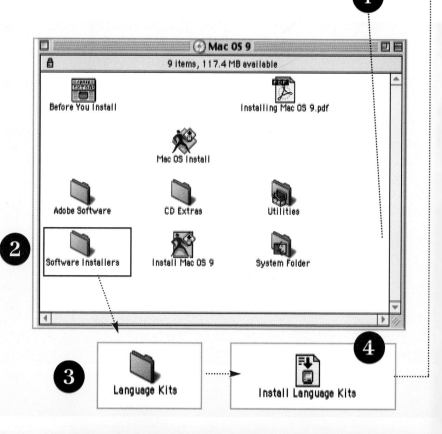

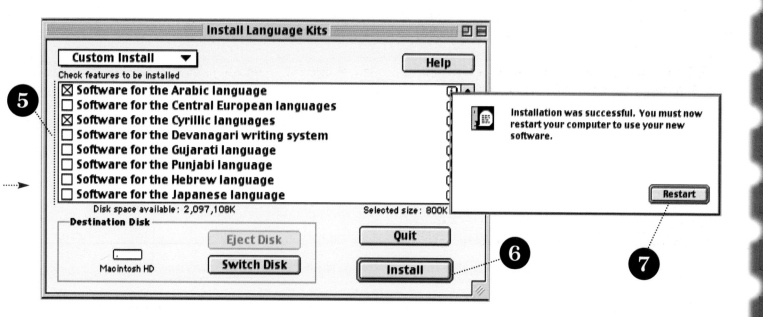

B. Installing the word processor, fonts and keyboard

① **Open the Mac OS 9 CD-ROM.**

② **Open the *CD Extras* folder.**

③ **Open the *Language Kits CD Extras* folder.**

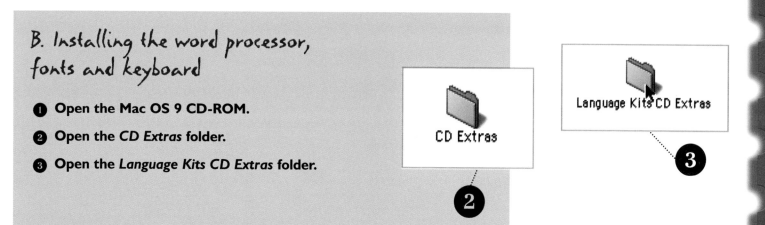

④ **Click the icon(s) of the alphabet(s) you want to install.**

⑤ **The program creates a virtual disk on your Desktop.**

⑥ **Open the virtual disk. It contains the following three items (more, if the alphabet covers more than one language):**
  - a *SimpleText* icon (for a word processor)
  - a *Fonts* folder (containing the fonts)
  - a *Keyboard* folder (containing the keyboard software)

⑦ **Copy the SimpleText application to a new folder (for example: LANGUAGES)**

⑧ **Install the fonts from the *Fonts* folder into the *System Folder*'s *Fonts* folder (see page 70).**

⑨ **Drag the keyboard from the *Keyboards* folder and drop it on the *Systems Folder*.**

⑩ **Restart your iMac.**

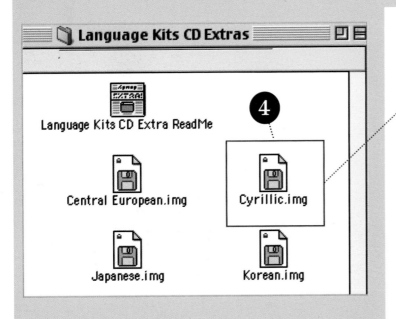

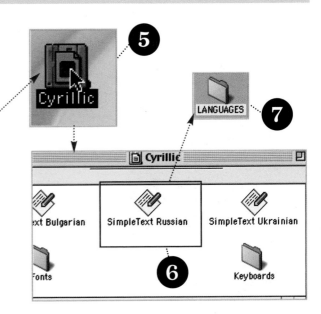

C. Using the word processor and the keyboard

1 **Open the selected word processor (here Russian)**

2 **Open the** *Keyboards* **menu and select the appropriate keyboard.**

Times New Roman
Trebuchet MS
TremorITC TT
Verdana
Wanted LET
Webdings
Бастион
Прямой
Ростислав
Системный
Latinskij
✓ PriamojProp
القاهرة
جيزة

The various fonts.

| йл | Редактор | Шрифт | Размер | Начертание | Звук |

| Отменить | ⌘Z |
| нованный |

Вырезать	⌘X
Скопировать	⌘C
Вставить	⌘V
Стереть	

| Выделить все | ⌘A |

Найти...	⌘F
Найти еще	⌘G
Найти выделенное	⌘H
Заменить...	⌘R
Заменить Еще	⌘D

На следующую страницу	⌘=
На предыдущую страницу	⌘-
На страницу...	

| Открыть Конверт | |

1

The SimpleText software application in Russian.

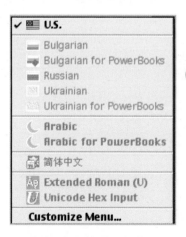

✓ 🇺🇸 U.S.

Bulgarian
Bulgarian for PowerBooks
Russian
Ukrainian
Ukrainian for PowerBooks

🌙 Arabic
🌙 Arabic for PowerBooks

简体中文

Extended Roman (U)
Unicode Hex Input

Customize Menu...

2

Note

When you restart the computer, the virtual disks will have disappeared from the Desktop. This is completely normal.

Troubleshooting

Like all Macintosh computers, the iMac is a reliable machine. It is not prone to crashing, and displays error messages only under rare circumstances (usually when there are extension conflicts: see page 72). Nevertheless, problems do arise at times, so it's best to be warned and to be prepared to pinpoint the cause of the problem rapidly.

A. My iMac isn't displaying the icons properly ...

... and no longer recognises the aliases, and seems to be experiencing memory and storage problems.

Don't be alarmed. There's simply a slight internal organisational problem within the iMac's database. Your iMac can no longer sort things out because the system has got into a mess for some reason. You can solve the problem by rebuilding your Desktop.

Notes

• Make sure that the Caps Lock key is not pressed before you do this.

• The Option key is also called Alt (for compatibility with the PC).

Rebuilding the Desktop

❶ Power your computer on and hold down the *Command* and *Option* (*Alt*) keys, until the following dialogue box appears:

❷ Click *OK*.

❸ The iMac will rebuild the Desktop in a matter of minutes.

Are you sure you want to rebuild the desktop file on the disk "Macintosh HD"?

Cancel   OK   2

CHAPTER VIII : APPENDICES

B. My iMac can no longer find the icons of the hard disk or the peripherals

It's as if they were no longer connected to the computer. Should I open my iMac?

You should do nothing of the sort!
It's probably a simple **PRAM** problem, as **PRAM** data at times conflict with the data on your iMac. You should reinitialise the **PRAM**.

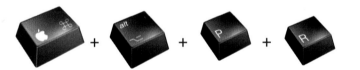

Reinitialising the PRAM

1 Power your computer on, holding down the *Command* and *Option* (*Alt*) keys as well as the *P* and *R* keys, until you hear the iMac sound identification twice.

2 The PRAM will now have been reinitialised, but your computer will have lost the preferences you'd set for certain items on your Desktop. The following items (at least) will have to be reprogrammed:

• **Memory**
• **Monitor** (and video cards)
• **Sound**
• **Keyboard**
• **Mouse**
• *AppleTalk*
• *Energy Saver*
• **Internet browser**

C. My clock is off every time I start up the computer

This is easy to solve. Replace the small internal battery that keeps the date and time. In theory, this should be done every five years, but for unknown reasons some batteries run down very quickly. This battery can only be replaced by your dealer.

D. My Mac has become very slow

This is merely proof that you're using it a lot. Don't worry: your machine isn't being run down. The reason it's slowing down is known as fragmentation. When your computer was brand new and your hard disk almost blank, programs could be written on it as a single block, and the computer could access them very quickly. As new files were saved and erased, however, large blank areas on your hard disk became rare. So files were kept 'fragmented' in several parts, wherever there was free space. And now, to find the entire file, your computer has to go over your hard disk several times and search in several places. This naturally takes time, and the performance of your programs shows it. You can solve this problem by defragmenting your hard disk.

Defragmenting the hard disk

The defragmentation process consists of regrouping separated blocks of a file. The iMac is not delivered with a defragmenter. However, Norton Utilities contains all the tools you'll need to defragment a sluggish hard disk.

E. Sound codes

Every time you start your computer, your system is subjected to a test. If anything abnormal is detected, the computer will indicate it with a number of beeps:

1 beep	Memory not detected.
2 beeps	Installed memory is not compatible with this model.
3 beeps	RAM did not pass the test.
4 beeps	There is a ROM problem.
5 beeps	There is a processor problem.

F. Error codes

These codes are very numerous and jealously guarded by Apple. However, there's a good list on the About.com site at

http://macsupport.about.com/compute/macsupport/
library/weekly/aa122099a.htm

G. About your computer

When the *Finder* is active (i.e. no other program is open on your Desktop), click the *Apple* menu, and then *About This Computer*. You can then see the following information about your iMac:

Built-in memory

Mac OS version

File   Edit   View   Special
About This Computer
🔲 Apple System Profiler

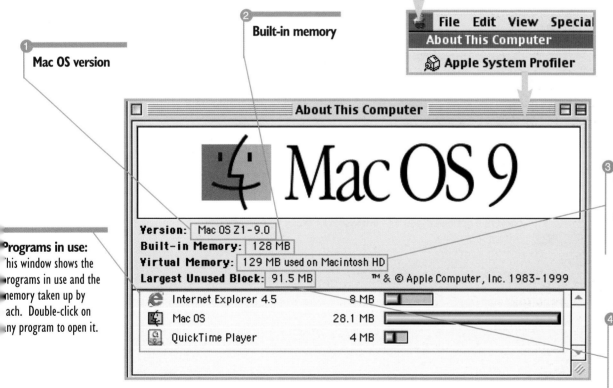

Programs in use:
This window shows the programs in use and the memory taken up by each. Double-click on any program to open it.

Virtual memory:
Memory used on the hard disk called 'Macintosh HD' (128 MB built-in memory + 1 MB virtual memory).

Largest unused block:
This helps you monitor the fragmentation of your disk. As soon as this figure falls below 5 MB, you should defragment the disk.

To find out more about the iMac OS team

• With the Finder in the foreground, click the Apple menu while holding down Command + Option + Control.

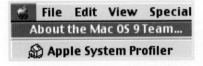

Instead of About This Computer, the option About the Mac OS 9 Team is now displayed.

Click this option to get a full-screen view of the names of all those who worked on the installed version of the iMac operating system.

• With the Finder in the foreground, click the Apple menu while holding down the Alt key.

Instead of About This Computer, the option About The Finder is now displayed.

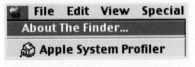

Click this option to view the names of all those who worked on the various Finder versions.

These small hidden programs are called Easter Eggs. There are hundreds that have delighted the programmers as well as those who discovered them.

Installing and reinstalling the operating system

If you have the iMac OS CD-ROM, installing the operating system is very easy, and you can opt to click *OK* as each installation screen comes up. However, you would then forego installing certain modules that may come in very handy (such as the language kit or the Web page designer). As the iMac is delivered without any documentation to speak of, to view these hidden treasures you'll have to explore the countless possibilities of the operating system when you install it.

A. Standard operating system reinstallation

❶ Double-click the *Mac OS Install* icon.

❷ Select your country.

❸ Click *Continue*.

❹ Click *Select*.

❺ Click *Reinstall*.

❻ Click *OK* in the various screens.

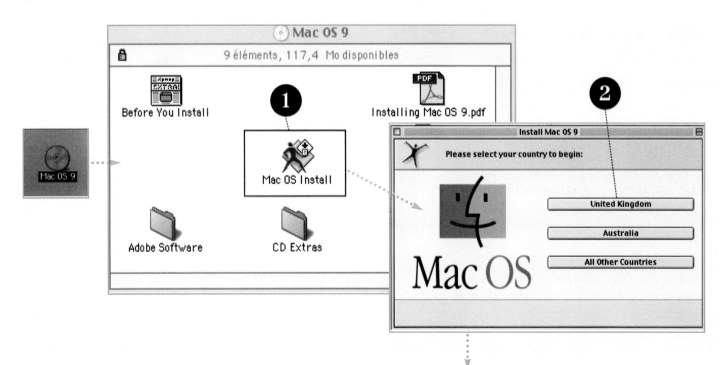

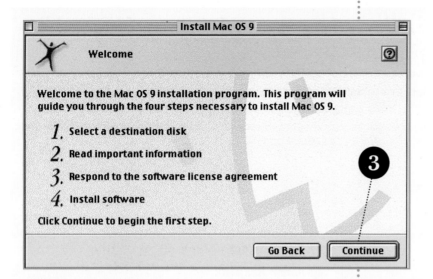

Note

Do not install all the programs, tools, drivers and extensions available, because your iMac might then refuse to restart (owing to extension conflicts). If this does occur, restart your iMac holding down the C key and with the Mac OS CD-ROM in the drive. The operating system will be launched from the CD-ROM. You can then either try to isolate the extension conflict (see page 74) or restart the installation process.

When restoring the system software, there are three options:

• *Restore, Saving Original Items*
• *Restore in Place*
• *Erase HD Before Restoring*

Select the first of these if you want to save the contents of your original hard disk files in a separate folder.

B. Custom operating system reinstallation

❶ **Open the Mac OS CD-ROM.**

❷ **Double-click the *Mac OS Install* icon and select your country.**

❸ **Click *Continue*.**

❹ **Click *Select*.**

❺ **Click *Add/Remove*.**

❻ **Tick the various modules you wish to install.**

❼ **Click on the installation mode icon of the first module to install, and open its menu.**

❽ **Select *Custom*.**

❾ **Tick the programs you wish to install.**

❿ **Repeat Steps 7 to 9 for each module you have selected.**

⓫ **Click *Start*.**

For screens number 1 to 3, see the screens of pages 149 and 150.

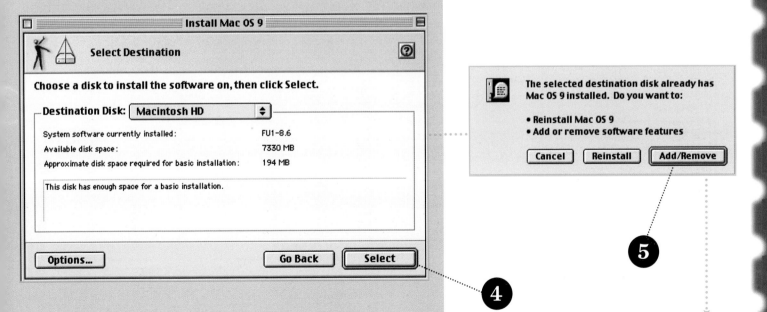

Install Mac OS 9

Custom Installation and Removal

Click Start to launch selected software installers on "Macintosh HD."

Software components	Installation mode
☑ Mac OS 9	Recommended Installation
☐ Internet Access	Recommended Installation
☐ Apple Remote Access	Recommended Installation
☐ Personal Web Sharing	Recommended Installation
☐ Text-to-Speech	Recommended Installation
☐ Mac OS Runtime for Java	Recommended Installation
☐ ColorSync	Recommended Installation

Don't Customize | Options... | Go Back | Start

Select Mac OS 9 features to install.

Selection: Recommended Installation

Feature	Size
☑ Core System Software	21,781K
▷ ☑ Assistance	5,366K
▷ ☑ Compatibility	948K
▷ ☐ Mobility	3,906K
▷ ☐ Multimedia	15,412K
▷ ☐ Network & Connectivity	17,656K
▷ ☐ Printing	9,965K
▷ ☐ Universal Access	45K
▷ ☑ Utility	7,216K
▷ ☐ Video	5,996K

Selected size: 107,625K

Cancel | OK

6

7

Select Mac OS 9 features to install.

Selection: Custom

Feature	Size
☑ Core System Software	21,781K
▷ ☑ Assistance	5,366K
▷ ☑ Compatibility	948K
▷ ☐ Mobility	3,906K
▷ ☑ Multimedia	15,412K
▷ ☐ Network & Connectivity	17,656K
▷ ☑ Printing	9,965K
▷ ☑ Universal Access	45K
▷ ☑ Utility	7,216K
▷ ☐ Video	5,996K

Selected size: 137,578K

Cancel | OK

8

9

11

Install Mac OS 9

Custom Installation and Removal

Click Start to launch selected software installers on "Macintosh HD."

Software components	Installation mode
☑ Mac OS 9	Recommended Installation
☐ Internet Access	Recommended Installation
☐ Apple Remote Access	Recommended Installation
☐ Personal Web Sharing	Recommended Installation
☐ Text-to-Speech	Recommended Installation
☐ Mac OS Runtime for Java	Recommended Installation
☐ ColorSync	Recommended Installation

Don't Customize | Options... | Go Back | Start

Glossary

ADSL

Asymmetric Digital Subscriber Line. Technology that allows high-speed access to the Internet using a telephone line.

AirPort

Technology used by iMac and iBook computers to implement a wireless network.

Alias

A shortcut represented by an icon that points to another file. Click on the alias and the corresponding file will open.

Application

Software designed for a specific task. For example, Word is a word-processing application.

Boot

The start-up sequence of the computer. During this operation the computer runs several different tests and, on failure of any of them, informs the user.

Bus

Set of electrical lines combined in one cable and terminated with a connector. Different buses are used to route data within the computer or between the computer and its peripherals.

Cache

Buffer memory which the computer uses to store data temporarily so that it can access it quickly if necessary.

Clipboard

Memory area used to temporarily store data that can be used by the current or another program.

Context(ual) menu

Menu that appears only at the user's request. It is specific to the context, i.e., to the operation being run.

Control Strip

Scrolling toolbar at the bottom of the screen. This toolbar contains different settings menus that can be accessed directly.

Desktop

The screen background on which windows, icons and dialogue boxes appear–in the way that a 'real' desk has folders and piles of work on it. The main screen of the Mac OS is also called a Desktop.

Dialogue box

Small window that displays useful information about the operation in progress.

Drag and drop

Technique consisting of picking up data by using the mouse and moving it to another location.

Driver

Tiny software that allows the computer to use a particular peripheral. Without installation of the driver, the peripheral will function improperly or not at all.

Ethernet

Technology that allows the connection of a number of computers and/or peripherals to create a local area network. The iMac/iBook come with an Ethernet connection which is often used to connect a printer.

Extension

Small programs that enhance the possibilities of the operating system.

Favourite

Folder that holds the addresses of favourite sites of the user. These addresses can be displayed, for example, with the help of the Favourites menu of Microsoft Explorer.

File

Set of data grouped together in one entity. A file can be a program, some text, some sound, etc.

File Transfer Protocol (FTP)

An Internet service (or protocol) that allows transfer (and downloading) of files between computers.

Finder

This is the graphic part of the Macintosh operating system. Finder is available at all times and is used for basic computer operations.

FireWire (or IEEE-1394)

Technology that allows the computer to communicate at high speeds with external peripherals that are also equipped with a FireWire port. This port is mainly used to connect video cameras, digital cameras or hard disks.

Folder

An entity for organising files in storage units (hard disk, diskette, etc.). The user can create as many folders as required and then place files inside them.

Font

Set of characters (letters, numbers, special characters) having a particular shape. These characters are used on the screen and for printing. The iMac comes with pre-installed character fonts but it is possible to add more to it.

Fragmentation

After some months of usage, each file is no longer stored in one place on the hard disk but is broken up and spread out over the disk. Access to data becomes slower. To defragment the disk and reassemble the broken-up files, a program such as Norton Utilities has to be used.

Frozen (program)
A frozen or crashed program is one that no longer responds to any command. To exit from it, it is not always necessary to reboot the computer (see page 66).

Hub
Unit that allows the connection of several peripherals to the computer; all the peripherals are connected to the hub which is itself connected to the computer. Since the iMac has only two USB ports, a hub is necessary to connect several peripherals, for example, such as may be required in a graphics environment (scanner, Zip, CD recorder, etc.).

Icon
Image representation of an object (file, program, sound, etc.).

Jaz
External storage device of large capacity (1 or 2 GB) using removable cartridges.

Kbps
Kilobits par second.
Unit of transfer speed used in the communications field.

Keyboard shortcut
Use of two or three keyboard keys to execute a command which would otherwise necessitate opening menus and use of the mouse.

Keychain
Mac OS 9 utility that allows the storage in one place of all access codes and passwords of the computer.

Local area network (LAN)
Sharing of resources of several computers and peripherals so that each user has access to them. Computers forming part of a network are usually connected by cables.

LocalTalk
Technology used by Apple to connect computers and peripherals in a small local area network. The iMac does not use this technology; it uses the Ethernet protocol instead. See Ethernet.

Plug and Play (PnP)
Describes a peripheral that is automatically recognised and configured by the operating system. It is only necessary to connect the peripheral to be able to use it immediately.

PostScript
A page description language. This language allows high-quality printing of images and text. Some fonts (called PostScript fonts), programs and high-end peripherals use this language. By using PostScript, the creator of a document is sure to obtain the best final quality irrespective of the PostScript printing peripheral used.

PRAM (parameter memory)
Small amount of internal memory in the computer that is used to store information about the system configuration. If the computer starts behaving erratically, this memory may need to be re-initialised (see page 145).

QuickTime
Software that adds multimedia capabilities to the operating system (Mac OS or Windows) and to Internet browsers.

RAM
Random Access Memory.
This is the main temporary memory inside the computer, one that is used by all programs. Its contents change all the time. The iMac comes with RAM of 32 to 128 MB (depending on the model) but the user can always increase the RAM by buying memory extension modules.

ROM
Read Only Memory.
This is the fixed memory inside the computer; its contents do not change.

Scrapbook
Compact software supplied with all Apple computers. This album allows the recording of objects such as text, 3D images or sound. Objects recorded in Scrapbook are available to other applications by simple Cut and Paste.

SDRAM
The new-generation memory modules. SDRAM is designed for use in the fastest computers.

Sherlock
A program incorporated into the Mac OS 8.5 and later versions of the operating system. It is used for searches on the computer and the Internet.

Shortcut
See entries for Alias and Keyboard shortcut.

SimpleText
Compact software supplied with all Apple computers. Initially this software was used only to read word-processing files. The latest versions are multimedia compatible and are available in several languages.

Stickies
A program used to create notes and to stick them on the computer Desktop (see page 79).

TCP/IP
Transmission Control Protocol/Internet Protocol.
Protocol used by all computers connected to the Internet. Nowadays, this protocol is configured automatically during the installation of any Internet software; users rarely have to concern themselves about it.

USB

Universal Serial Bus.
System for connecting computer peripherals.
This system has several advantages and was
thus chosen for the iMac (see page 103).

VGA

The minimum graphics display standard for a
computer. VGA mode allows the display of 640
x 480 pixels in 16 colours. Several other
standards, based on the VGA standard, are
more powerful.

Virtual Disk

Creation of an area in the main memory that
will be treated like a hard disk. This allows you,
for example, to download data from an external
disk into the main memory and thus speed up
access to it.

Virtual Memory

The use of part of the hard disk as supplemen-
tary memory when the main memory is
insufficient. In this case, the program transfers
some rarely-used data to the hard disk
(swapping).

Window

The basis for any graphical interface
(see page 43).

Zip

External storage peripheral that uses large
capacity (100 or 260 MB) removable cartridges.

Index